D1372945

Reflections
—OF— THE SOUTH

Reflections
OF
THE SOUTH

Bethany Ewald Bultman

GALLERY BOOKS

Text
Bethany Ewald Bultman

Design
Alan Hamp

Research Assistant
Anne Strachan

Editorial Assistant
Elizabeth Greene

Photography
FPG International
Black Star

Photo Editor
Annette Lerner

Project Director
Sandra Still

Dedication

To my parents, who brought me up
southern.

To my Yankee husband who takes
great pleasure in the eccentricities
and complexities of Southern life.

To my sons in hopes that their
Southern values will always bring
them joy, and make them thoughtful
citizens of the world.

To all the Southern blues singers who
make the world a sweeter place.

Acknowledgements

A thoughtful note of appreciation to
Sandra Still for her friendship and
support. Special thanks to all of the
museum directors, archivists and
friends who have shared their
southern heritage, especially to Ann
Belkov, Julia Webb Bland, John
Bridges, Lucy Buffett, Rosanne Cash,
Lucy Core, Karl Ewald, Ann Masson,
Peggy Neilson, Tim Pickles, Susan
Norman, Bryce Reveley, Jim Roberts,
Macon Riddle, Walton and Molly
Rutherfoord, Liz Thiels, and Alice

VIRGINIA

KENTUCKY

NORTH CAROLINA

TENNESSEE

SOUTH
CAROLINA

ARKANSAS

GEORGIA

MISSISSIPPI

ALABAMA

LOUISIANA

FLORIDA

CONTENTS

Above: *Michigan Monument, Vicksburg National Military Park, Mississippi.*
Right: *the Blue Ridge Mountains near Greenville, South Carolina.*

Introduction

The history of the Old South has a lot to do with how the New South has manifested itself. It has been said that the New South is like an ancient live oak with sprawling limbs and a broad trunk, which has been battered by the elements, but with a tap-root buried deep in southern history. Culturally, socially, and politically the South is a definite force, wily and sometimes fickle. One thing is for certain, southerners have perpetuated and preserved the ideals, traditions, and myths that sustained them through good times and bad. The South resonates with associations: some literal, and others symbolic, sensual, and emotional. It is the cradle of America's music – the blues, bluegrass, jazz, rhythm & blues, and country.

The South has been called a country within a country. Here life is a bit quirkier, more romantic and more fanciful. Rhetoric and laughter come with the territory. A true southerner is pleasurably conscious of who he is, though he won't bat an eye at transforming anecdote into legend and legend into truth. The gracious ho-hum gallantry is just one of the many layers that set southerners apart.

It was in the sultry South that the history of the United States began many years before the Pilgrims landed at Provincetown, Massachusetts, and later moved on to Plymouth Rock and points west. This was where Spain's powerful galleons sailed the waters of the Gulf, seeking gold, the fountain of youth, and adventure.

The Spanish flourished in the area from South Carolina to Florida. In 1650 there were approximately

Above: *musicians playing near Boone, North Carolina.*

300,000 people living in the region of South Carolina. Only about 10,000 spoke English. Long after their language ceased to be predominant, the cultural roots of Spain remained.

A hearty breed of dedicated men and women from throughout Europe were crucial to the future of the South in those two hundred years after Jamestown. Farmland had to be wrestled from the wilderness, forests had to be cleared, trees had to be felled, and stones and roots had to be wrenched from the earth. The harsh and bloody task was accomplished with bent backs, parched skin, and callused hands by men, women, and children. The men would push the plow while the women toiled with the hoe. During planting season, families would work all night with women and children holding the pine torches. Those who worked the hardest were able to grow the most, earn the most, and buy more property. To sustain larger tracts of agricultural land, more laborers were needed. Early

Above: russet-roofed farmhouses in the lush, autumnal farmland of Virginia.

Right: Gideon Shyrock's Old State House in Little Rock, Arkansas.

on it was discovered that the native Americans would rather die fighting than be enslaved. Most were unfriendly and hard to catch, and they were rather adamant in their refusal to work the land that had been stolen from them in the first place.

With prosperity came the wherewithal for the farmers to charter convict labor from England and later to buy slaves. Sustained by a dream, a tenacious and lucky few ended life as elder statesmen in white-columned mansions. For most the impoverished life was a continuation of the downtrodden existence they had left in Europe. These relentless settlers rejected the rigid structure of New England Protestantism in favor of the goal of building empires and fortunes. With very few exceptions, there was no

high-minded justification like that of the Pilgrims in New England, who embraced the ideals of the yeoman farmer and freedom from religious persecution. Early southerners knew they must battle the elements – thunderstorms so fierce they could wash out a field in an hour, deadly fevers, ferocious heat, and loneliness, but they knew that success was a possibility.

By the advent of the American Revolution in 1776, seven generations of colonists had spread throughout the southern coastal regions. Prior to the 1820s, the distinctions between rich farmer and poor farmer were virtually unnoticed. Cities were scarce. Life was sustained by the soil, and the outdoorsmen of the emerging culture grew to manhood whooping it up with the "fellas" on coon hunts and drinking raw, rot-gut whiskey. For the majority of those who survived past the age of thirty, life ended with little more than a few hard-won acres and a one-room log house, which exemplified nothing more than muscular simplicity and freedom.

By 1830 the wealthy landowners began to spread out, pushing the poor farmers to the undesirable back-country, which sold for less than a dollar an acre. These early Virginia and South Carolina settlers had made tobacco fortunes and, using the landed aristocracy as role models, had quickly created a gentry to mirror the lordly class of England. By the late 1830s, they had depleted their tobacco lands and had seen most of their English tobacco market evaporate. Many Virginia gentlemen had to take their genteel manners, English educations, and whatever money they had left to live among red bugs and mosquitoes in new territories such as Alabama, Mississippi, and Florida in order to rebuild lost fortunes.

The society the fortunate few established was even more feudal than the ones in Europe from which they had fled. During the years between 1820 and 1860, the South became more than a mere geographical locale. It was in this short period that its previously untrodden frontiers were transformed by cotton blossoms to a paradise resplendent with silver doorknobs, damask curtains, crystal chandeliers, and tall white pillars. In the South the former peasant could rise to great heights by reaping the benefits of black slave labor.

This was all made possible by a Yankee schoolteacher from Yale, Eli Whitney, who found the way to extract tiny cotton seeds from the recalcitrant fiber. The cotton gin was invented in 1793, and by 1860 about five million bales or two-thirds of all American cotton was produced in the Deep South east of the Mississippi River. By the 1820s those farmers with luck and will were hard at the task of letting cotton turn them into kings. Growing cotton was a labor intensive operation. Of course, within these

years there were bad crops, droughts, hurricanes, fear of slave uprisings, bankruptcies, epidemics of fevers, and the Great Panic of 1837. Yet grand as this legendary period of southern history was, scholars have speculated that there were probably no more than four or five thousand families of real wealth in all of the South.

One English traveler of the period explained that the distance between plantations was "big enough to dump a European country into and lose it without a trace." Gracious hospitality became legendary, with guests staying for months of balls, picnics, supper parties, and weddings. Yet during the same period, many of the slaves had so little contact with whites and so little education that they could hardly speak English. Their society was as aloof and savage as the land itself, causing a majority of the white aristocracy to fear for their lives.

Between the time when John Quincy Adams became President in 1825 and the secession of eleven southern states from the Union in 1860-61, there was also a growing economic tension and animosity between the North and South. Slavery became the emotional lightning rod. Without the "peculiar institution," the large-scale production of cotton,

Facing page: *stalks of foaming, cotton-bearing buds in a field near Florence, South Carolina.*

Right: *a reenactment of the Battles of Manassas, outside Manassas, Virginia.*

Below: *the tomb of the unknown soldier who fell at Vicksburg, Mississippi.*

sugar, and rice would be impossible. At the same time the North began to experience an industrial boom. The South became, to use Allen Tate's phrase, "Uncle Sam's other province."

The peculiar institution of slavery had bonded African-Americans with the white gentry so strongly that each had come to provide the half of the whole that was the South. The children of the upper society were generally brought into the world by a trusted black midwife. Infants of the white household were suckled by a black wet nurse and lovingly ministered to by a black mammy. Their childhood companions were slave children; their mentors were the "Uncle Remus" storytellers and black "bosses," who taught them to hunt and ride. The black cook was the friendly confederate, who smuggled them sumptuous treats between meals and taught the daughters of the family secrets of household management.

Whether from the Ivory Coast, Angola, Mauritania, or Senegal, the slaves found themselves systematically segregated from tribal alliances, languages, and customs, and forced to adapt to cultures as varied as the French Creole sugar planter and the Anglo-Virginian, nouveau-aristocratic tobacco farmers.

Not all southerners liked the idea of slavery. To the dejected Catholic Highlanders, who had fled Scotland after the defeat of "Bonnie Prince Charlie," forced labor in any form was repugnant. They chose to live primarily in the hills and mountains of Georgia, the Carolinas, Tennessee, and Kentucky. In the period between 1760 and 1770, the Highlanders of North Carolina became the chief protagonists of the "Regulator" revolt against the English governor and Tidewater planters. This served as a principal catalyst to the Revolution; yet when the Revolution came, many of the same men decided they preferred to support the Crown of England over the proud slaveholding gentry next door in Virginia.

During the Civil War the Ozark region of Arkansas sent 8,000 men to the Union Army, while the northeastern hill country of Alabama sent 3,000. East Tennessee, the Cumberland region of Kentucky, western North Carolina, and the hill country of South Carolina and Georgia also supplied many men to the anti-slavery Union Army. This, however, did not mean that these southern folks were any less "southern" in their culture or that they suffered any less during Reconstruction.

The die-hard descendants of the old plantation

An old horse-drawn wagon in eastern Tennessee.

society will never refer to "the War," i.e., "the War between the States," "the Late Unpleasantness," or the "War of Northern Aggression," by the term used by historians – The Civil War. To say "Civil War" discounts the fact that the Confederate States of America was a separate nation, however short-lived.

It was this war and its aftermath which would definitively dictate what the South was to become. For several decades after defeat, the southern states were cut off, almost frozen in time. Two to three generations in each family felt the direct effects of the death of father, brother, son, or beau. Many had their homes looted or burned, their land stolen by carpetbaggers or through taxation, and their stores looted, or crops burned. Pride, defeat, poverty, rage, shame, frustration, and hunger were powerful forces, which molded a culture glorifying a pre-war past that grows more and more romantic in retrospect.

It wasn't until after World War I that the northern establishment reembraced the South and its culture. This isolation nurtured a powerful creativity. The world heard its potent voice in everything from literature and music to Coca-Cola, Pepsi, and the airplane. Many a southern town was saved by southern matrons who realized that a "Yankee tourist was worth more than two bales of cotton and was twice as easy to pick." Pilgrimages and tourist attractions still abound throughout the South today.

In the rural south life was hard. After the end of slavery, an equally unfair system of sharecropping evolved, which economically enslaved the lower classes, both black and white. The Mexican boll weevil did to the cotton plantation system what war and depression could not. It forced crop diversification.

The twentieth century brought the onset of a rigid caste system that is somewhat blurry to the outsider. At the top are the descendants of the old pre-war money. Although being truly rich is not a criterion for upper class, breeding is. This class is just small enough that there is always someone who remembers exactly who everyone's grandfather was, where he lived, and how he made his money. One rather telling parameter is how leisure time is spent. Those who

Facing page bottom: *costumed townsfolk following troops reenacting the Battles of Manassas in Virginia.*

Above: *Louisiana's bayous, "a maze of sluggish and devious waters," in Longfellow's words, provide habitat for alligators.*

educate their well-groomed children, have well-tended flower beds, and perform good works for the less fortunate are "good solid folks" (pronounced like good salad *forks*). As the expression goes, "They may be too poor to paint and too proud to whitewash, but they keep the place tidy."

On the other hand, those who loll about under trees, slap their dirty-faced "chillun" in public, and exhibit sloppiness while inebriated are known as "white trash." These folks were characterized as the Snopes family by William Faulkner. W. J. Cash in his renowned 1941 study, *Mind of the South*, states that this underclass enjoyed a "half-thrifty, half-shiftless prosperity – a thing of sagging nail fences, unpainted houses and crazy barns which yet bulged with corn." Politically, this group is known as the "Bubba Factor." If they vote, they vote conservative; they drink wet and vote dry. The southern middle class of today is made up of those who raised themselves up from the lower class through education, good deeds, and

money and those who have fallen from the upper class through lapses in breeding.

Southern women, whether rich or poor, black or white, are a breed unto themselves. Beneath their grace and poise there is the "iron fist in the velvet glove." Plantation ladies ran the household, planned the meals for dozens, doctored slaves, and did it all in five pounds of flowing skirts and expertly coiffed hair. The character of Scarlett O'Hara showed the world what the southern lady was made of.

The geographical area defined as "the South" has an infinite variety of terrain: there are rolling hills, riverbanks, palm-lined white beaches, low-lying swamps, piney woods, fertile black delta lands, unrelenting red clay fields, and mountains. The economic and social differences between the southeastern and the southwestern states are vast. As the land was settled, immigrants from various parts of Europe gravitated to certain kinds of land. Relatives, friends, and compatriots found it easier to follow the vanguard settlers once language and customs had been established.

Throughout the South there are long growing seasons; hot, humid summers; and gentle winters. Nowhere else in the United States does a people tie their mythology and symbols to nature as integrally as do the southerners. At the core of the mythology of the South is the Mississippi River. The great coils of the powerful, gleaming river move to the Gulf, having carried generations of Indians, explorers, flatboat men, river steamers buried beneath story-high bales of cotton, barges, tugboats, and oil tankers. It is the artery and the lifeblood that has transported cotton, sugar, indigo, rice, lumber, oil, and grain to the world markets. The Mississippi is the largest river in North America. It feeds the fertile Mississippi Valley and Delta, which were created by the river's 1.25 million-square-mile drainage area. The river touches two Canadian provinces and thirty-two states on its winding path to the Gulf.

Hernando de Soto, in 1541, is credited with being the first European to see the river, and later it became his grave. The French followed, and by 1717 were building levees in an attempt to control its force. In Natchez, Mississippi, all but one street of the famed Under-the-Hill section was carried away by the ever-changing course of the river. Floods continue to challenge the Army Corps of Engineers, who maintain over 1,700 miles of levees, floodways, reservoirs, and dams.

The Live Oak, the state tree of Georgia, is so closely linked to the mythology of the South that a registry has been created for them. The trees are native to the south Atlantic Coast from Virginia to Florida and along the Gulf Coast to Texas. It is called the live oak because of its tenacious qualities. The Indians used the plentiful acorns for food, for sweet oil, and as a powder similar to cocoa.

Where would any southern gothic novel be without its cliché of "moonlight and magnolias?" The magnolia, the state flower of Mississippi, has mammoth, sweetly fragrant white blossoms and is native from Virginia to Texas. In the summer, fireplaces are filled with deep-green, shiny magnolia branches to hide the blackened hearths.

Kudzu is a prolific cousin of the bean family, which the Japanese introduced to the South at the New Orleans Exposition in 1884. Since then it has quietly been taking over the hills and valleys. Back then it seemed like the ideal, hearty vine to shade loggias. By the 1950s it had caught hold with a force right out of a horror movie. In the summer it can grow up to a foot a day, smothering everything in its path from trees to

Below: *the* Natchez, *one of New Orleans' famous river boats.*

Above: *live oaks near Grand Chenier, Louisiana, draped in burnt-sienna colored foliage.*

Right: *St. Paul's Episcopal Church on East Queen Street, Pendleton, South Carolina.*

houses to automobiles. State road commissions and military installations use it to prevent erosion; some people feed it to cattle; and the Japanese make a nutritious powder from it. Southerners do have a sense of humor about the vine, however. In Chattanooga, Tennessee, there is an annual Kudzu Ball on the same night as the prestigious Cotton Ball. The Kudzu Ball is funky, loud, and held to raise money for Chattanooga's Birth Defects Center. All participants, especially the Kudzu King and Queen for the evening, must be attired from head to toe in kudzu.

Spanish moss is the brooding thread that runs through poems, stories, and legends; hangs from tree limbs in eerie tatters, taking on the shapes of ghosts; and lies across fallen branches in diaphanous blankets. Cajuns in Louisiana use it to stuff mattresses, and the Indians still make baskets from it. Journalist James Kilpatrick sees Spanish moss as a metaphor for the South: "An indigenous, an indestructable part of the southern character, it blurs, conceals, softens, and wraps the hard limbs of hard times in a fringed shawl."

Moss is an epiphyte, a plant with no roots, which lives off moisture in the atmosphere. It is an air plant (*Tillandsia usneoides*) and a cousin to the pineapple. Tiny scales on the moss's tendrils trap rain to keep

moisture from evaporating, and stems can grow twenty-five feet long. The Choctaw Indians called it "falling hair," the Spaniards called it "Frenchman's wig," and the French referred to it as the "Spaniard's beard."

The area predominantly occupied by religious fundamentalists in the South has been labeled with the term "Bible Belt." Bible-Belt values do speak loudly throughout much of the South. Politically, a state like Louisiana is always fascinating because the Catholics of French, Spanish, and German descent in the southern part of the state see life very differently from the Bible-Belt Baptists of Anglo-Saxon ancestry in the north.

In the beginning, most of those who came to the South were fairly tolerant of the religions of others. This was a rural society engrossed in the problems of daily survival. Anglicanism in reality seemed confined to the wealthy pre-Revolution seaboard districts and pockets of rich planters in areas like Virginia and low-country Carolina and Georgia. It has been noted that there were about 50,000 Episcopalians in the entire South at the outbreak of the Civil War.

The staunchly Presbyterian Scotch-Irish were certainly another formidable force. Generations before, these people had been brought to Ireland from

15

Scotland as laborers by English landlords, who disliked the Catholic Irishmen. They were both denigrated by the English and detested by the Irish.

But by the early nineteenth century the hardworking farmers sought a faith that could soothe the soul, calm fears, and provide social order. Tent-rocking revivals were one of life's highlights in rural areas. Charismatic preachers, who rose from the ranks of the downtrodden agrarian stock, bedazzled them with an apocalyptic God full of demands and redemption. Soon Methodists and Baptists were gaining in numbers. During Reconstruction and the Depression, religion provided the only glimmer of hope for many individuals. The preacher was called upon to dictate politics as well as morals.

Heat and dealing with heat during the summer has always been a major concern in everything in the South but fashion. Fine ladies and gentlemen have always followed the strictest code of elegant attire, no matter what the temperature. Much of the architecture reflected the methods employed by the Spaniards and planters in the Indies, who raised their houses off the ground, created high ceilings which allowed the hot air to rise above the living area, and constructed long, covered verandas where interior furniture was placed during the daylight hours. Dining rooms were supplied with punkahs, which were gently fanned back and forth to keep the flies off the food while cooling the diners. In the hottest part of the day, a large meal was served, after which the shutters were drawn, and the family members retired to their beds for a nap.

The very wealthy were able to get ice, which was wrapped in straw and stored in caves. Upon occasion, proper ladies would have buckets of it placed beneath caned-seat chairs, and would disguise their personal air-cooled compartments under their voluminous skirts.

With the advent of railroads in the late nineteenth century, northern businessmen were able to transport ice quickly to the eager, sizzling southern market. Blocks of winter ice were packed in sawdust, and soon horse-drawn ice wagons were doing a booming business in the southern towns served by railway depots.

Ice cream, which had been a favorite of Thomas Jefferson, was now available to the masses. For an "uplifting" cooler, some ingenious citizens simply cut a plug out of a chilled watermelon, and filled it with a bottle of "white lightning."

Electricity brought the use of ceiling and rotating fans. The wealthy could put blocks of ice in front of a fan for "cooled air." By the mid-1930s, air conditioning was a luxury reserved primarily for first class railway

cars and picture shows. Within a decade air conditioning had changed the climate of the South. Prosperous banks, offices, hotels, and restaurants provided their privileged clients with cool air. The 1950s brought air-conditioned automobiles and window units for homes. This invention was partially responsible for the South's becoming the new frontier for those northerners seeking sunshine and moderate winters.

Since the early eighteenth century, southerners created methods to help them coexist with the multitude of insects. Gilded mirrors, picture frames, and chandeliers were covered in mosquito netting to prevent flies from laying eggs and creating black spots. Upholstered furniture was swathed in linen slipcovers to protect the fabrics. Beds were encased in mosquito netting. Yet with all of the knowledge of protecting possessions, the settlers never realized that it was these same vermin that spread deadly fevers. Window screens were introduced in the late nineteenth century, but it was not until the turn of the century that it was proven that insects caused disease.

To truly know the southerner, one must eat his food. The passionate sense of life that goes with the hot, humid climate is nowhere experienced more poignantly than at that cultural font, the southern dinner table. The Civil War could start all over again in a debate over the "right" way to fry chicken. There are as many methods as there are cooks in the South. And, yes, there are really familial feuds as to which flavor dessert is better – pecan, chocolate, lemon, or custard.

Facing page: *San Francisco Plantation Home at Garyville, Louisiana.*

Above: *hot chili peppers at a farmers' market in North Carolina.*

Above: *the lush swamps of Georgia support a wide variety of wildlife.*
Right: *a black fret of trees near Gainesville,*
powdered with freshly fallen snow.

Georgia

The name of Georgia conjures up a variety of diverse images. On one hand there is its capital, Atlanta, which is also the standard bearer of the New South. On the other, this is the land which is as much of a character in Gone with the Wind, *the definitive tale of the splendor and sadness that was the Old South, as Scarlett, Rhett, Melanie, Ashley, Mammy, and Prissy.*

A look at a partial list of the celebrities born in the state illustrates this complex legacy. The contributions of Georgians to the development of rhythm & blues is remarkable. Performers Little Richard, Ray Charles, Gladys Knight, Otis Redding, and James Brown all hail from this state. Other musical native sons include Kenny Rogers, Brenda Lee, Harry James, and Ma Rainey. Comedians Oliver Hardy, of Laurel and Hardy, and Nipsey Russell and actors Ossie Davis, Kim Basinger, Stacy Keach, Jr., Jim Brown, Burt Reynolds, and Joanne Woodward are all Georgia-born. Both writers Alice Walker (*The Color Purple*) and Joel Chandler Harris (*Uncle Remus*) came from the heartland of Georgia; and Eatonton was the home of Flannery O'Connor.

To many sports enthusiasts Georgia is known for the Masters Golf Tournament in Augusta each April; to

Above: *evocative relics of Savannah's antebellum past.*

Georgia

Civil War buffs it is where Confederate President Jefferson Davis was captured by Union troops in Irwinville on May 10, 1865. Americus/Plains gained worldwide prominence as the small agricultural home territory of former President and Nobel Prize winner Jimmy Carter. But perhaps few outside of the state remember that Georgia was also where aviation pioneer Charles Lindbergh made his first solo flight.

Historically Georgia has a unique and colorful past. The skeleton of an early Georgia resident, a forty-five-million-year-old archaeocete whale found in Burke County, sits in Statesboro as a reminder of the region's ancient aquatic history. The mammal is a companion to the Mosasaur, a "colossal fossil" that swam in the seas of the area seventy-eight million years ago.

Generations of Indians inhabited Georgia for some 10,000 to 15,000 years before Europeans got interested in the area. The first white men were sailors from Wales, Ireland, and the Scandinavian countries, who stopped over to enjoy the beauty of the region. The Spaniards who arrived in 1540 made the most lasting

Below: *a formation of thick, bolster-like clouds spread over fields near Cleveland.*

Facing page: *a low, winter sun backlights a dense filigree of fishing nets off Georgia's coast.*

impression, leaving behind missions and fruit trees. By 1566 they had established Franciscan missions on St. Simon's and Jekyll islands and along the coast of the mainland. The French arrived about the same time, but they left little. They did take sassafras, the root in root beer and the herb used to make filé powder, turkeys for King Louis' table, and a small fortune in animal skins.

In 1717 Sir Robert Montgomery, a Scottish knight/real estate developer, distributed broadsides to possible settlers extolling a paradise on earth. He was Georgia's first public relations man. He wanted to turn the flat plain along the coast into the fiefdom of Margravater of Azilia, with himself as lord.

After the land had been tried out for a few hundred years by these short-lived visitations, James Edward Oglethorpe, his visionary English settlers, and some of the victorious British soldiers who had turned back the Spanish at Bloody Marsh created an English colony to buffer the English territories from the Spanish in Florida. Oglethorpe was a philanthropist with high-minded ideals, which included a desire to live peacefully with the Indians and to produce crops without the use of slaves. He convinced King George II to let him have the vast tract of land that stretched from the Carolinas to Spanish Florida. He further reasoned that he could alleviate British prison overcrowding by taking non-violent criminals with

Right: *a cotton harvest brings to mind Foster's nostalgic lines: "Gone are my friends from the cotton fields away."*

Above: *a fountain on Factor's Walk, along the Savannah River.*

Left: *the evening sky transforms Savannah's skyline into a gauze of mists and smoke, curling around the finely etched, black lines of industry.*

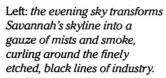

him. Debtors, political dissidents, and convicts were given over to him as a labor force to produce wine, spices, and silks for the English market. The theory was that these new indentured servants would gladly work in return for their eventual freedom. He argued that all temptation to fall back into crime was removed, since alcohol was banned from the colony.

He and his cargo of settlers landed in 1733 and set about creating Savannah, a city which was soon to become a gracious metropolis of parks, plazas, and shaded streets. By 1749 idealism had given way to the competitive spirit, and slaves were imported to expand the indigo, rice, and cotton-growing potential of the newly emancipated English freedmen. A few

years later the charter of Georgia reverted to the British Crown, and vice reared its little curmudgeon's head. On January 2, 1788, it became the fourth state to ratify the United States Constitution.

Georgia's plantation aristocracy flourished until the Civil War, when it felt the full force of the North's rage. The name of General William Tecumseh Sherman still stirs a spark of rage in most Georgians. Two months after his burning Atlanta in September of 1864, he and 60,000 Union troops began their infamous march to the sea. He announced his desire "to make Georgia howl." The only exception is said to have been one tiny town outside of Atlanta where Sherman's college roommate's family lived. As he stated, "We are not fighting armies, but a hostile people, and must make old and young, rich and poor, feel the hard hand of war . . ." Savannah, which he didn't burn, was his Christmas present to Lincoln. Along his route the genteel fabric of Georgia was not only tattered, but trampled. His troops raped, pillaged, and burned houses and crops; they stole food and livestock; they even sewed salt in the soil so that crops would not grow for decades. Thus the tragic war was to end where the proud will of the southerner had begun, in the low country on the coast. In the aftermath of Sherman's march, hundreds of freed slaves and their ex-masters were left to starve.

The Georgian response to degradation was to rebuild the state's capital in Atlanta. The phoenix was chosen as the city's symbol; "Resurgence" as its

Facing page: *the Cathedral of St. John the Baptist, built in Savannah in 1873, is Georgia's oldest Catholic church.*

Below: *Road Atlanta, ten miles south of Gainesville off State 53, a SCAA-sanctioned road course for Grand Prix racing.*

motto. On the capitol building, dedicated on July 4, 1889, is a remarkable gilded dome and cupola made from Georgia gold. One year after the end of the Civil War, the population of Atlanta was double what it had been before the fire. Its Confederate history is honored at the 3,200-acre recreational and historic park of Stone Mountain. The mountain itself is the largest piece of exposed granite in the world, measuring about two miles in length and seven miles in circumference, reaching 825 feet above the plateau base. It features a 90 by 190-foot-high relief sculpture of Confederate President Jefferson Davis, General Robert E. Lee, and General "Stonewall" Jackson, each astride a horse. It took over fifty years and three sculptors to finish the elaborate monument.

Not only was Atlanta the administrative center for Reconstruction, but it was also the forerunner in the establishment of schools for former slaves. By the turn of the century, it had created a strong class of black professionals. On January 15, 1929, Martin Luther King, Jr., was born there, and in 1973 Maynard Jackson became mayor of Atlanta and the first man of African descent to be elected to lead a southern city.

The phoenix is an apt symbol for Atlanta's strides in the American Civil Rights Movement. The spiritual leader of the movement, Dr. Martin Luther King, Jr., spent his youth in Atlanta, and is buried near the Martin Luther King, Jr., Center for Non-violent Social Change and the Ebenezer Baptist Church, his and his father's church. They are located in the Sweet Auburn Historic District, a late-nineteenth-century black professional area. This section boasts of the nation's

first black-owned commercial radio station, WERD, and includes the headquarters of the Southern Christian Leadership Conference. The nearby Atlanta University Center is a world-renowned consortium of historically black institutions, which have provided both inspiration and education for many of the leaders of the African-American community. These include Clark, Atlanta University, Morehouse, Morris Brown, and Spelman.

The mega Coca-Cola empire is synonymous with Atlanta. In 1886 an Atlanta druggist named John Pemberton, who sought a remedy for headache, mixed an extract of sugar, cocoa leaves, cola nuts, and cocaine in a pot in his backyard. Within a year his drugstore had dispensed twenty-five gallons of the refreshing brew. That same year another druggist

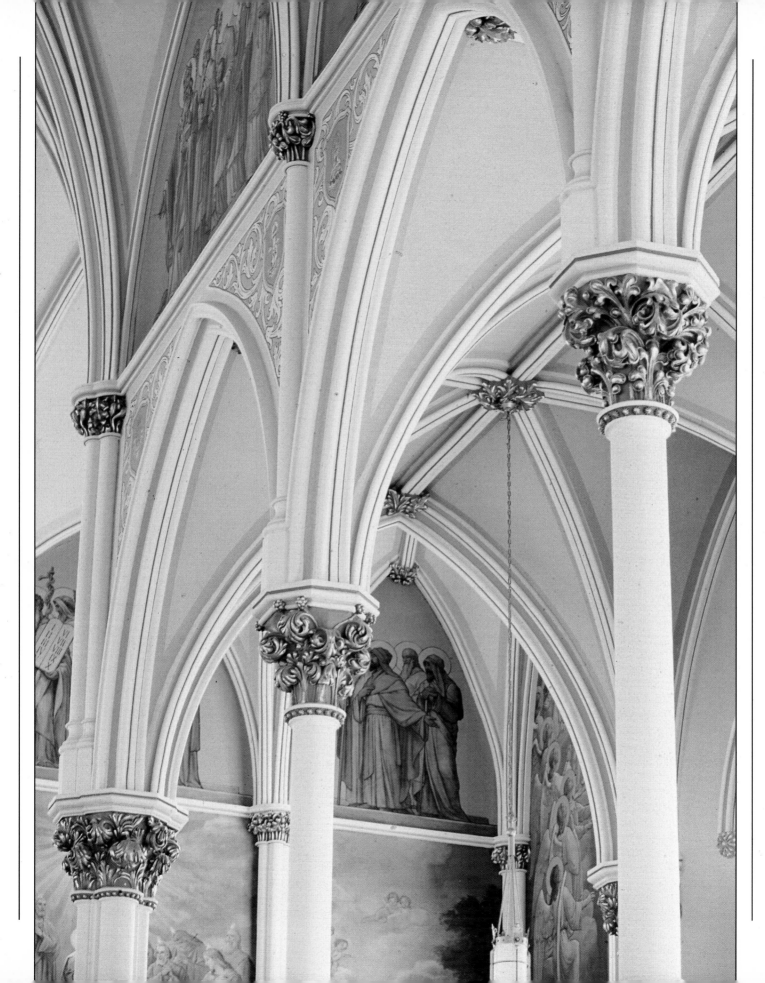

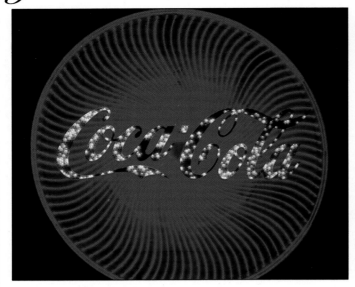

Above: a neon advertisement, the modern face of Atlanta.

mixed some carbonated water with the Coca-Cola, adding the sparkle beloved by the world. In 1891 a third druggist bought all the rights to the Pemberton formula for two thousand dollars. Today the Coca-Cola empire includes an extensive multinational corporation, which controls a variety of businesses including Hollywood studios.

The original Pemberton formula is a closely guarded secret known only to three men in the world. It is kept in a safe-deposit box in the Trust Company of Georgia. The magic ingredient is called FX. The only things that have been revealed are the facts that the formula no longer contains cocaine and that corn sweetener has been substituted for sugar.

Atlanta is the New South. It is the largest city in the South, both in population and number of industries whose headquarters are there. It is estimated that four hundred of the Fortune 500 companies have offices in Atlanta. The national headquarters of the Centers for Disease Control (CDC) is also located here. The Atlanta airport is one of the largest airline hubs in the world. The saying goes that even to get to heaven a traveler has to go through Atlanta. Atlanta was the site of the South's first radio and television stations, WSB radio and later WTBS-TV. Today it is the home of maverick media entrepreneur Ted Turner's cable television empire.

Seventy miles to the southwest near the large granite quarries is the famous Callaway Gardens, noted for its flowers and its exceptional stone-ground grits. Located at Pine Mountain in the foothills of the Appalachians, the opulent gardens are the handiwork of the late Cason Callaway, who in 1938 set about to replenish the red soil of his family's 2,500-acre cotton plantation. The garden contains one of the world's largest collections of native azaleas from the

perhaps partially accounts for the state's vitality. The town of Dahlonega, whose name means "yellow metal" in Cherokee, was originally called Licklog until it became the site of America's first goldrush. Here the Federal Mint coined millions of dollars from the town's gold mine from 1838 until the Civil War.

In 1835 an itinerant stonecutter, traveling on a remote path in the backhills of north Georgia, noticed an outcropping of fine marble. He founded a quarry on the site. Today this Jasper vein has been estimated to be large enough to supply the world's building needs for hundreds of decades to come.

The Georgia low country is flat, nearly sea-level land with dazzling white beaches and mysterious sea islands, shaded backroads arched over with ghostly, moss-draped trees, and spectral ruins in overgrown fields. The coastline once bloomed with cotton; then timber became a prime money-maker. Then the early twentieth century brought about destruction, poverty, and the boll weevil. Once fertile farmlands became wild and tangled.

These sparsely inhabited islands, whose only inhabitants were tribes of ex-slaves who spoke the Gullah dialect, became prime hunting land for the privileged, who came a few times a year. A consortium of millionaires from the Northeast and Midwest bought Jekyll Island in 1886 for $125,000. The Rockefellers, Pulitzers, Astors, Morgans, and Cranes created a southern hammock-rocking, golfing outpost, a Deep South Newport that survived until the 1940s. Today the beguiling natural beauty and robber baron architecture draw tourists year round. The manicured fairways and sixty-three holes mark the state's largest public golf resort.

Today a maze of narrow bridges, lagoons, and inlets separates the mellow palmetto- and oak-fringed, white sand beaches of the sea islands from the mainland. In an area the size of Manhattan, St. Simon's Island has long been a retreat for the privileged of South Carolina and Georgia. The English had sailed south from Savannah to the island in 1736 to build Fort Frederica, which still stands on the secluded, snake-like curve of the Frederica River. It was to this remote area that Aaron Burr fled after mortally wounding Alexander Hamilton in a duel.

Sea Island itself lies across a slender strip of marsh from St. Simon's Island. Here since 1928 generations of southern aristocrats have summered at the Cloister, a Spanish-style resort.

The coastal plain stretches 35,000 square miles into Georgia. The fertile land, once seabed, extends from the 435,000-acre Okefenokee Swamp to the slash pine area near Augusta. The Okefenokee Swamp is one of the last natural swamps in America, occupying much of the southeastern corner of the state and reaching into northern Florida. The Suwannee, as in

Facing page bottom: *the fragile beauty of an azalea bloom in the Callaway Gardens, one of 700 varieties to be found there.*

Above: *a party of vacationers enjoying the tree-canopied tranquility of Cumberland Island National Seashore.*

southeastern woodland areas. Over 700 types of azaleas are grown here, including rare specimens of yellow, orange, and red varieties. In 1988 the Day Butterfly Center, named for the founder of Days Inns of America, was opened here. It is the largest glass-enclosed butterfly conservatory in North America and contains over 1,000 tropical butterflies, who weave a kaleidoscope-like pattern as they dive, climb, dip, and spin against the sky and sun. Robin Lake has the largest man-made white sand beach in the world, and the John A. Sibley Horticultural Center houses a fascinating indoor/outdoor conservatory featuring acres of flowers and a two-story waterfall.

The fact that Georgia is so rich in natural resources

Stephen C. Foster's immortal song, "Way Down upon the Suwannee River," and St. Mary rivers flow through the shallow, 950-square-mile basin, renewing the terrain for a wealth of plants, fish, birds, and animal life. Tall, dense strands of gnarled cypress are interspersed with flat, open prairies dotted with patches of vegetation. The Seminole Indians called the area the "Land of the Trembling Earth."

The midland section of the state boasts a bountiful array of agricultural treasures. It is from this area that the Vidalia sweet onion comes. Millions of stately pines yield timber and turpentine for markets all over the world. Many of the southeast's largest cattle ranches are located in the Magnolia Midlands, and the town of Claxton hosts the Rattlesnake Roundup, as well as a multitude of world-famous cake bakeries.

The rolling Piedmont peaks near Atlanta, gradually sloping to the southeastern part of the state. Georgia's largest river, the Chatahoochee, serves as the lower Georgia-Alabama border. The Oconee, Ocmulgee, and

Facing page: *the Blessing of the Shrimp Fleet at Darien.*
Right: *swimmers in the Chattahoochee River.*
Below: *an enticing platter of seafood caught off Georgia's coast.*

Above: *a floating sun speared by the rushes of Moon River.*

Right: *the pillars of an old Georgian home, trellised with wisteria.*

Below: *a wooden hut reclaimed by the wilderness of Georgia.*

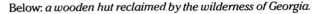

Savannah, which marks the Georgia-South Carolina border, all originate from this area. The water from many of these rivers flows to the Gulf of Mexico.

The Appalachian "uplift" dominates the northern part of Georgia. Brasstown Bald, the highest point in the state, is 4,784 feet above sea level. This isolated region, thick with hardwood trees and encompassing 749,444 acres, is the Chatahoochee Forest. In the northwest part of the state is the mountainous ridge and valley country which is linked to the Alleghenies and Cumberland Plateau. The cooler climate here is reminiscent of the mountains in North Carolina.

Each Georgia town has a personality of its own. One-half of the world's tufted carpets come from Dalton's 200 carpet mills; Hoschton, with the introduction of the Alberta peach in 1875, also has the noted Chateau Elan Winery; Fort Valley has been the peach center of the "peach state," which is the largest producer of peaches in the world. It is also the national headquarters of the American Camellia Society and the Stevens Taylor Gallery, where over 300 rare Boehm porcelain sculptures are on display.

Facing page: *the Wagner Fruit Stand, Alto.*

Above: *surfers ride the Atlantic waves on Myrtle Beach on The Grand Strand.*
Right: *lights bejewel the walls of Harbortown on Hilton Head.*

South Carolina

The border between South Carolina and North Carolina is twofold: there is the natural frontier and then there is the point where the inhabitants languish just a bit more. To lump the Carolinas together is like matching a chestnut horse with a horse chestnut. Each is a distinct cultural entity. South Carolinians like to say that their state is less a location on a map than a way of thinking.

Within the state there are three distinct geographical regions: the low country/coastal plain, the Piedmont, and the Appalachian Mountains. The inhabitants of each are fiercely clannish. Until the nineteenth century, the middle of the state was Indian country, which was a natural barrier between up-country and low country. The Savannah River, which flows through J. Strom Thurmond Lake, Richard B. Russell Lake, and Hartwell Reservoir, creates South Carolina's border with Georgia. At the northwest corner are the Blue Ridge Mountains, which separate South Carolina and North Carolina.

Today tobacco and cotton are first and second in importance to South Carolina's agricultural production. The largest industry, however, is the manufacture of textiles, and the second largest is tourism. Fruit harvesting is also important. McBee is a

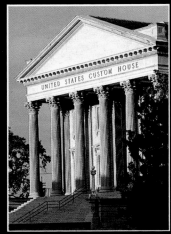

Above: *the United States Custom House, Charleston*

tiny community renowned for its cultivation of grapes used in the making of wine. The world's largest peach-shipping center is located in Spartanburg, also noted as one of the southern centers of textile production.

Both Vasquez de Ayllon and Jean Ribault attempted to settle the area of South Carolina in 1526 and 1562, but little was to come of this. The area was rediscovered by English explorers in 1663, and it was soon to become the province named for the ship *Carolina,* which brought the first English settlers. The landgrant from the British Crown indicated that the lands were to run all the way to the Pacific Ocean. They included what is today South Carolina, North Carolina, north Florida and northern Georgia. The first settlement was on a peninsula embraced by the Cooper and Ashley rivers at Albemarle Point in 1670, and was named by the Prince of Wales, later King Charles II, Charles Town. After the Revolutionary War, American patriots changed the name to the less British Charleston.

The first settlers, all 148 people, brought indigo seeds, ginger roots, sugar cane, olives, fruits, and vegetables with them. In the 1680s the first French Huguenots arrived, driven out of their homeland by the revocation of the Edict of Nantes, which from 1589 to 1685 had given them restricted religious and civil liberties. Soon afterward, Captain John Thurber sailed into the Charles Town harbor, bringing with him Madagascar rice. By the eighteenth century, rice was

Facing page: the 182-foot-high steeple of St. Michael's Church in Charleston.

Below: a lancing tournament held in Charleston's Middleton Gardens.

A distorted view through old glass in a Charleston house.

so important that it was used for currency, "Carolina gold."

One of the South's most important women was a South Carolinian, Eliza Lucas, the teenaged daughter of the British governor of Antigua. She arrived in South Carolina in 1738 and, by the time she was seventeen, she was running her family's plantation. Prior to her experiments, no one had been able to produce a satisfactory indigo-blue dye in America. She discovered a strain of the plant and a method of planting that revolutionized the production of indigo. Her discoveries were soon to make her and many other South Carolinians very rich indeed. Many years later President George Washington served as one of her pallbearers.

Indigo even proved to be more profitable than rice, although the creation of the highly priced blue dye had a deadly by-product. Large vats of water were required, which bred mosquitoes, which, in turn, spread deadly fevers. There was a saying that "Carolina is in the spring a paradise, in the summer a hell, and in the autumn a hospital."

The South Carolina low country around Charles

Above: *against a salmon-colored sunset two people fish off Charleston's Battery.*

Left: *an elegant, underlit fountain epitomizes the grace of Charleston.*

Right: *the Citadel Museum depicts and displays the history of the Military College of South Carolina.*

Town was soon crowded to overflowing with colorful characters – buccaneers, slavers, spies, and deserters. Blackbeard wreaked havoc in the port of Charles Town in the early 1700s. While such individuals are the fodder for legends, many of them don't provoke the same pride among southerners as do the forefathers of colonial Virginia. Mixed into this exotic stew were English Puritans, who had rejected the rigid communities of New England, Swiss planters from the Indies, and the Dutch.

Between 1710 and 1740, the black slave labor force far exceeded that of the white planters. As early as 1708 there were as many blacks as whites. In the rural areas slaves outnumbered whites by sixty to one. This was the largest slave concentration in the New World. Fear of slave uprisings was an ever-present concern.

The city of Charles Town was to become one of the largest, most important, and most sophisticated cities in the colonies of the New World. Vast low-country plantations along navigable water routes sprang up so quickly that large tracts of overgrown wilderness had to be bypassed, making distances between plantations extreme. Stately mansions along the Ashley River still maintain some of the most extensive and glorious gardens. The streams that veined the area all led to Charles Town, creating a cosmopolitan refuge for the planters. Isolation and fear led planters to build imposing town houses near sea breezes to escape the scorching, malarial low-country summers.

In the eighteenth century, Crevecoeur called Charles Town the most brilliant of American cities. He raved that the city had a society second only to London. A journalist published an account of white society in a 1773 article in the *South Carolina Gazette and Country Journal* which states, "Every tradesman is a merchant, every merchant is a gentleman, and every gentleman is of the noblesse. We have no such thing as common people among us. Between vanity and fashion, the species is utterly destroyed."

The country's earliest zoning laws were passed in Charleston in 1929. In 1947 the Historic Charleston Foundation was created to preserve the city's magnificent historic architecture. Of all of America's colonial cities, Charleston has preserved more of its fiber and essence than any other in North America. The walled gardens and iron gates lend a Mediterranean flavor, while the Dutch influence is shown in the exquisite tile work and the French, in the long, narrow lots. Eighteenth- and nineteenth-century Charlestonians came to refer to their city as the "Little London" or the "American Venice." Expert artisans educated in England maintained rigid standards, providing some of the finest examples of pre-Revolutionary brick architecture and post-Revolutionary Chippendale and Adam/Federal-style buildings.

Throughout the Battery, the city's harbor area, are convex roof tiles, stuccoed walls, and overhanging balconies, which illustrate a definite mixture of Barbadian and Huguenot influences. Buildings reflect the West Indies in their sunbleached palette of salmon, peach, rose, blue, saffron, and celadon. First floors were raised off the ground for coolness and protection against flooding. Most Charleston houses are still built with the same Creole/Indies components that satisfied the seventeenth- and eighteenth-century settlers' needs for ventilation.

The Citadel, "the South's own West Point," is another Charleston institution, having survived since 1843. It was a group of hot-headed, young cadets from the Citadel who fired upon a federal steamer three months before General P. G. T. Beauregard's troops fired on Fort Sumter, thus initiating the War between the States. On December 20, 1860, South Carolina was the first state to pass the Ordinance of Secession. The small community of Abbeville is credited with being

"The Birthplace of the Confederacy." It was the location of the first secession meeting and the place where the Confederate cabinet had their final meeting in 1865.

The Confederate attack on Fort Sumter in Charleston harbor on April 12, 1861, marked the beginning of the Civil War and the end of an era of prosperity in the South. One-fourth of all the South Carolinians who fought in the war were killed. The state's motto, *Dum spiro spero,* "While I breathe, I hope," reflects the spirit of the survivors.

Charlestonians have long had a rigid sense of decorum. Society maintains a gracious insularity with old-line families still enjoying the century-old tradition of three o'clock dinner. The ultimate debutante presentation in the South, if not in the entire United States, is that of Charleston's St. Cecilia Society. Named for the patron saint of music, it was formed in 1762 to give concerts and still thrives today, though very discreetly. So very private and proper is the club that neither it nor its ball, where debutantes are presented, is ever to be mentioned by participants. Many old Charleston families who have been excluded pull down their window shades the night of the ball to prevent anyone from knowing that they are not among the elite members.

The low country continues to foster culinary inventions unique to the area. The Charlestonians have a preference for eating the sweeter female crab in a luscious cream sherry-flavored soup, called she-crab soup, and they like their oysters roasted. The slaves who arrived in the seventeenth century brought sesame seeds (benne). Today they are used in everything from stews to biscuits.

The urban low-country accent might just sound "southern" to a Yankee, but to a southerner the accent is an evolved eighteenth-century British colloquial drawl, refined and blurred by damp, drink, and diet. Gardens are called "gyardens." Coastal and island-dwelling blacks, having lived isolated lives as slaves, developed their own unique dialect. Called "Gullahs," many of this group still speak a mishmash of African and English, and eat a cornbread dough called "cush."

Seen from the air, the low country appears as a somnolent forest of cypress, pines, and oaks hung with melancholy tatters of moss and a splash of climbing vines. The soil which gave birth to the

Above: *the 200th Anniversary reenactment of the Colonial Muster – the first Southern land battle of the Revolution.*

Facing page: *Fort Sumter, from which the opening shots of the Civil War were fired, at the entrance to Charleston harbor.*

Right: *the 200th Anniversary reenactment of the Colonial Muster held on the "96" National Battlefield.*

Left: *cypress trees rise in tall shafts rise from the waters of Charleston's Cypress Gardens.*

The State House in Columbia is the only structure on Main Street that predates the burning of Columbia in 1865. Begun in 1851, it is constructed of blue granite quarried locally.

41

low-country fortunes is a sandy loam, the air so thick it can almost be seen. The coastal land area is dotted with seductive fertile islands seaward: the turquoise sea, with a metallic silver light on it, and the shadowed jigsaw of marsh and shore look as though they would fit together.

Hilton Head Island is the largest island between New Jersey and Florida. It is twelve miles long and up to five miles wide, and is bordered by one of the last major unpolluted marine estuaries on the coast. It wasn't until 1956 that a bridge to the mainland was created. Within years it had become one of the most popular resorts in the world. It has jokingly been called South Jamaica because it is the southern American version of that Caribbean island. Throughout the island, the boom and hiss of the

waves can almost be drowned out by the mutter of golf carts and the thud of tennis balls.

Between the low country and the up-country lies Columbia, the capital of South Carolina since 1786. It is located approximately one hundred miles northwest of Charleston, and was named for Christopher Columbus. In 1801 the University of South Carolina was chartered here. At the turn of the century, one of the first all-electric textile mills in the world began operation here, thus revolutionizing industry. Columbia was also where future President Woodrow Wilson lived with his parents, the Reverend Joseph Ruggles Wilson and Jessie Woodrow Wilson, while his father taught at Columbia Theological Seminary and was minister at the First Presbyterian Church.

The Piedmont up-country area has a different

Above: *the elegant interior of the 1854 Lace House on Richland Street, Columbia.*

Above right: *a tower of South Carolina's University, the Horseshoe, in Columbia.*

Right: *students practising an Oriental martial art in the grounds of the University of South Carolina, Columbia.*

A lively class in a school at Rock Hill.

Above: *the colorful bulbs of competing hot air balloons rise from a site near Greenville.*

Facing page: *the inky rigging of boats moored on a calm evening at Mount Pleasant.*

pedigree from the low country. In the early 1730s, while the low-country folk were enjoying a life of luxury, fiercely independent Scotch-Irish, Welsh, German, and Kentucky and Pennsylvania settlers took over the remote higher elevations of the Piedmont Plateau. Much of the earth underfoot was hard, red clay. By the early nineteenth century, these tenacious settlers had created cotton empires, which made them far richer than the low-country residents.

By the 1840s the up-country's York County had one of the highest per capita incomes in the nation. Camden is the oldest town in the region, founded in 1733 by Irish Quakers. It was a place where low-country folks would come in the summers to escape the fevers and hot weather near the coast. Today it possesses one of the largest historic districts in the state. Its Springdale Course is the site of one of the South's most famous steeplechase facilities.

Aiken, the "Polo Capital of the South," is currently the southern oasis for the New York horse crowd. It became an "in" place more than a century ago when "sickly" robber barons came to inhale its dry, pine-scented air. They created Long Island-style architecture and formal gardens, which still abound. In 1872 W. C. Whitney and Thomas Hitchcock built one of the first golf courses in the South. And the rest is history!

Above: *the Columbus Statue in Reston, Fairfax County.*
Right: *the Front Royal National Zoo incorporating the Front Royal Breeding and Conservation Center.*

Virginia

To the rest of the South there is an aura of aristocracy and homeland about Virginia. Of all of the original thirteen colonies, Virginia is the oldest. It was also Britain's oldest colony in North America.

While other southerners might have trouble determining whether a person is from Alabama or Arkansas, Virginians are easy to pick out. They speak with an accent that is, while not British or southern, distinctly Virginian. About is pronounced "aboot;" house is "hoose." It is the sort of eccentricity that southerners respect. The history of Virginia and its statesmen is also nice to claim kin to. While Virginians still proudly trace their motivations to the eighteenth century, they recently became the first state in the nation to elect a black governor. That's one thing about being an old matriarch like Virginia is: she can and will do whatever she damn well pleases. But whatever she does will be done with decorum and good taste.

To know this stately lady, one needs to realize

Above: *the dome of Colonial Williamsburg's Capitol*

Above: *a white, clapboarded house with dark shutters.*

where she came from. Sir Walter Raleigh was a prisoner in the Tower of London in December of 1606, having fallen from the favor of his Queen, Elizabeth I. On that winter morning he witnessed three vessels setting forth for Virginia: the *Susan Constant*, the *Godspeed*, and the *Discovery*. The virgin land where they were headed was named Virginia after his Virgin Queen. Sadly, most of the one hundred men and four boys would be dead within a few months. The food supplies were rapidly depleted, and their storehouse was filled with "as many worms as grains."

The village of Jamestown, which they founded on May 13, 1607, was chosen as a good point for defense. Unfortunately, it was a low point where the heat of summer blistered down and river water stagnated; and in the winter it was so cold that the fish froze in the river. It served more as a breeding ground for mosquitos than for drinking. The early settlement in Virginia became a hell of dysentery, typhoid, dissent,

Indian attacks, and starvation. Two years after its founding, 440 of the newly-arrived 500 inhabitants had died.

After twenty years the London Company had sent 7,250 settlers, of whom 6,000 had died. Once in the new world, a settler was likely to survive for six months. Records show that women and hogs survived better than men and dogs, though there was a report of a man who killed his wife, salted her, and stored her for daily nourishment. 1619 was a banner year for the surviving settlers. Over one thousand emigrants came from England. These new colonists included a shipload of young ladies chosen by the Virginia Company as potential wives. In order to get a wife, a man simply had to pay passage for the lady of his choice in tobacco. This was similar to the deal offered the indentured servants, except the wives weren't offered freedom after seven years.

From 1624 until the American Revolution, Virginia

Left: *an undulating field in Virginia, traced by a wooden fence and stone wall.*

Above: *a stream flowing through Virginian woodland carpeted with fallen leaves.*

was one of the English Crown's favorite and most prosperous colonies. It was originally quite large, as evidenced by the states that were later formed from bits of its land: the Carolinas were broken off in 1629, Maryland, in 1632; after the Revolution, Kentucky, Ohio, Indiana, Illinois, Michigan, and Wisconsin; and during the Civil War, West Virginia.

The English settlers who had moved into the Tidewater had made peace with the new land by 1705. In that year historian Robert Beverly described the landscape, "Their eyes are ravished with the beauties of naked nature. Their ears serenaded with the perpetual murmur of brooks. . . . Their taste is regaled with the most delicious fruits. . . . And their smell is refreshed with an eternal fragrancy of flowers."

Contrary to what straight-backed, aristocratic Virginians like to say about their ancestors, most of those who came from England to Virginia were fleeing poverty. Unclaimed land was sometimes granted to freed indentured servants; when settled, it served as a buffer between the class of British officials and the Indians.

Had not Sir John Rolfe married the Indian princess, Pocahontas, to insure peace with the Indians, the Virginia settlers may have given up the experiment in colonial living. The new friendship with the Indians also taught them how to cultivate a marketable strain of tobacco – a weed which the Spanish had brought to Europe in the fifteenth century as a cure for hangovers and gout. With the export of the first crop in 1614, the life of the tenacious settlers changed. Almost immediately it made these suffering settlers so rich that starvation and disease no longer seemed that much of a problem. As the British market for tobacco expanded, so did the price, and within a few seasons hardy young farmers were able to amass great wealth. Tobacco was the principal crop that provided the wealth. By 1619 a strong-willed, democratic assembly

had been set up to protect the interests of the new class of Virginia gentlemen farmers.

The farms along Virginia's four great rivers – the James, the York, the Potomac, and the Rappahannock – were prime areas because they were deep enough for ocean-going ships. The lucky farmers who had these riverfront or low-country tobacco, rice, or indigo farms were quick to send their sons to England to university to achieve the education which had been denied to their parents. By the early 1700s these Virginia-born sons were returning home with polished notions and aristocratic ideals. To fit in with the British society they so admired, these educated Virginians of the pre-Revolutionary period set about to build monuments to elevate themselves beyond the station of their illiterate, laboring parents. Good taste became crucial; homes must be fashionable, both inside and out. Virginians relied heavily on books from England to tell them what was *au courant*. It wasn't until the second half of the eighteenth century that the first dining rooms appeared, illustrating when manners and graciousness had caught up with wealth.

The diet of the Virginians is a close copy of Continental cuisine. One of Virginia's earliest ice-cream devotees was George Washington, who had a "cream machine for making ice" installed at Mount

Above: *Shirley Plantation standing southeast of Richmond on the James River.*

Facing page: *Gunston Hall, begun for George Mason in 1755 near Lorton.*

Vernon. During the summer of 1790, accounts show that Washington spent approximately two hundred dollars on the frosty delicacy. Thomas Jefferson, who is supposed to have developed a passion for ice cream while in Paris, was the first president to bequeath an ice cream recipe to the nation, one he had acquired in France.

Plantation life was self-contained. Tobacco or indigo was the cash crop, while grains, vegetables, fruits, and livestock were grown to sustain the master, his family, and slaves. It is thought that southern graciousness came from this isolation. Guests became welcome on sight. These visits made the pursuits of fox hunting, horse racing, and balls possible. House parties could last for weeks. Unlike the pilgrims in New England, eighteenth-century Virginians preferred communication with each other to religious devotion to their maker.

Tobacco had two serious by-products: soil depletion and slavery. It quickly depleted the minerals in the soil so that farmers needed bigger plots of land. By the late eighteenth century, all of the good land in

Virginia had been bought up. Twenty blacks were brought to Jamestown from the West Indies by a Dutch warship in 1619. While the first blacks were indentured servants, by the 1640s Jamestown had a thriving slave market. At the same time, the Virginia Company auctioned off white indentured servants. In Virginia between 1710 and 1750 the black population grew from 10,000 to 100,000 to service the massive plantations.

Williamsburg was established as the center of "court" life in the colony. While most planters resented the aggrandizement of the royal governors appointed by the king, they could, however, see the need for a sophisticated, ceremonial city where they might live for a portion of the year. Furthermore, the money for the "palace" came from local taxes. Thomas Jefferson called the town "the finest school of manners and morals that ever existed in America," though he felt that the city's architecture was much too "British colonial" for his taste.

This was the town where the United States got its beginning. In May 1776 the Virginia Convention urged the Continental Congress to declare the colonies independent of the rule of the British Crown. By July the Virginia Declaration of Rights had been drafted, which would serve as the basis for the Bill of Rights. By the beginning of the Revolution, the spate of

Left: *the Governor's Palace in Colonial Williamsburg, begun in 1708 and finished in 1720.*

Right: *the Capitol, Colonial Williamsburg, a replica of the first Capitol of 1705.*

Above: *Tuckahoe Plantation, seven miles west of Richmond.*

aristocratic decadence was to stop. Historian Daniel Boorstein has called the American Revolution "the suicide of the Virginia aristocracy." Once free of English rule, the tobacco trade collapsed.

Colonial Williamsburg of today covers 173 acres of the original eighteenth-century town of Williamsburg, the capital of Virginia from 1699 to 1780. Patrick Henry, George Washington, and Thomas Jefferson once walked the streets and planted the seeds that would grow into the Revolution. Thomas Jefferson was the last governor to live here, because in 1780 the capital was moved to Richmond.

In the 1720s Colonial Governor Spotswood built a new Governor's Palace in Williamsburg that outdid everything Virginians had seen in the colonies. The palace was designed in the English baroque style by Sir Christopher Wren. Brick had replaced wood as the favored material; out was the seventeenth-century superstition that stone houses caused disease. The new palace extolled an order and elegance that bespoke the aristocratic life that was and still is Virginia.

The sleepy, decaying old capital was rescued in 1920 by the late John D. Rockefeller, Jr. Today it is visited by over a million people annually. The second-oldest college in America, Willam and Mary, is located in the city of Williamsburg adjacent to the historic area.

The Virginia statesmen are credited with having fired the other colonists with their hatred for British rule and their vision for an independent nation. Prosperity had created a small core of Virginians determined to rebel against the British by 1676. After the defeat of the British a hundred years later, Virginians led in the framing of the Constitution, and gave the nation four of its first five presidents. Virginia today honors its many historical figures and their homes – George Washington, Thomas Jefferson, Thomas Lee, Stonewall Jackson, Patrick Henry, James Monroe, Woodrow Wilson, and Booker T. Washington.

Thomas Jefferson, the third president of the United States, is the favorite son of Virginia and the United States' most famous Renaissance man. He was a statesman, a scholar, an inventor, an architect, a botanist, a lawyer, a philosopher, and a gourmet. Of

all the historic homes of Virginia, Jefferson's Monticello is one of the grandest. It sits atop an 867-foot hill two miles to the south of Charlottesville. During his years of service to Virginia and then as a minister to France, secretary of state, vice president, and president of the United States, Monticello was his refuge. His personal delight in designing and refining his home was a lifetime passion. From 1769 until 1809 he molded a new symmetrical American architecture from a variety of classical elements. It was at his home that Jefferson died on July 4, 1826, on the fiftieth anniversary of the Declaration of Independence.

There is but one university in the mind of a Virginian. Mr. Jefferson saw his dream of an "academic village" with the laying of the cornerstone of the first building at the University of Virginia on October 6, 1817, in Charlottesville. Jefferson wanted to create a school that would bring enlightenment to education and would serve as America's first secular college. The campus was created on an open court with a magnificent view, suggesting the limitless

Above: *a wrought-iron gate in Monticello emblazoned with "TJ" for Thomas Jefferson.*

Facing page: *Monticello, Thomas Jefferson's home from 1809 to 1826, when he died.*

possibilities of education. He took his inspiration for the architecture from the classical. The Rotunda was patterned after the Pantheon in Rome.

Charlottesville is in the rolling foothills of the Blue Ridge Mountains. It was notably the home of Thomas Jefferson, but also of James Monroe and explorers Meriwether Lewis and William Clark. Albemarle County is in the heart of Virginia's fox hunting country, and is where the succulent Albemarle Pippin apple was first bred.

The Tidewater of Virginia is the lowland area which extends as far inland as the tides reach. This coastal plain is the eastern fourth of the state, though it is still referred to by its historical name. The

The elegantly laid out gardens of Jefferson's Monticello.

Above: *the Blue Ridge Mountains, Virginia.*

Left: *the State Capitol, Richmond, by Thomas Jefferson and C.L. Clérisseau.*

Right: *a lone cannon stands against a dark, evening sky on Manassas National Battlefield.*

Above: *the University of Virginia, Charlottesville.*

Chesapeake Bay and its tidal rivers produce an abundance of seafood, especially crabs and oysters. It was here in Westmoreland County at Stratford Hall that the family who has made the greatest impact on the South lived. The house was built in the late 1790s by Virginia's first native-born colonial governor, Thomas Lee. Five of his sons played crucial roles before and after the Revolution, with two of the brothers being signers of the Declaration of Independence. Their cousin, General Henry Lee, called "Light-Horse Harry," famed Revolutionary War cavalry commander, governor of Virginia, and eulogist of George Washington, lived here beginning in 1782. On January 19, 1807, his second wife gave birth to future Confederate General, Robert E. Lee.

Virginia was not on the front lines of the secessional movement that led to the Civil War. A state convention held in Richmond in April 1861 voted two to one not to join the Confederacy with the seven southern states that had already seceded. The convention reversed itself when Lincoln demanded that they take up arms against the South. Its native son, Robert E. Lee, became the Confederate Army's commander, and its capital, Richmond, was chosen as the second capital of the Confederacy, because of its location. Richmond was a major producer of iron and was in the center of a rich agricultural area.

The White House of the Confederacy was located in the house of a prominent Richmond doctor and financier. It was while living here that Confederate President Jefferson Davis's five-year-old son was killed when he fell from the east portico. Another problem was the Davis's black maid, who was hired on the recommendation of one of Richmond's most prominent matrons, Elizabeth Van Lew. It was later discovered that Mrs. Van Lew was a high-ranking Union spy, and that the maid was one of her agents.

Virginia's proximity to the North made it the principal battleground of the Civil War. Richmond, its women, and all of its buildings were soon involved in the care of hundreds of thousands of Confederate wounded. The fall of the nearby city of Petersburg led to the fall of Richmond on April 1, 1865; a week later Lee surrendered at Appomattox.

The war had a devastating effect on Virginia. Its leadership was defeated, many of its men were dead or maimed, much of its land and most of its crops were destroyed, its economy was in shambles, and one-third of its land had become the State of West Virginia.

Richmond's Hollywood Cemetery is the final resting place of American Presidents Monroe and Tyler, Confederate President Jefferson Davis and eighteen thousand Confederate soldiers. A difficult time followed, yet Virginians knew that the Old Dominion would prevail. Their pride and knowledge of their Virginia identity provided an anchor during years of humiliation and economic instability.

The Virginia of the twentieth century has been rejuvenated by another dynasty, this time the Byrds. In the 1920s Governor Harry F. Byrd set in motion policies that pulled Virginia into the industrial revolution. The activation of ports such as Norfolk and Newport News and the preparation for World War II put the state back into a position of leadership. Today the Hampton Roads area is the home port of the Atlantic Fleet and twenty-two other strategic naval commands. Newport News Shipbuilding is one of the world's largest private shipyards. Also, a large portion of Virginia is closely tied to the federal government.

Arlington is a thriving suburb of the nation's capital, Washington, D.C. Located there is one of the world's largest office buildings, the twenty-nine-acre Pentagon, a five-sided structure which houses the Department of Defense. The Arlington National Cemetery was established in 1864 on land confiscated from General Robert E. Lee. Many famous Americans lie here, including former President John F. Kennedy, Robert Kennedy, Rear Admiral Richard E. Byrd, Supreme Court Justice Oliver Wendell Holmes, Jr., General John J. Pershing, fighter Joe Louis, and the Unknown Soldier. His tomb is carved from a fifty-ton piece of marble, one of the largest pieces of Colorado marble ever quarried.

While tobacco is no longer Virginia's main crop, it is still very important to the economy of the state. The cigarette, and in particular The Philip Morris Company, breathed life into Richmond's productivity. Danville is one of the most active tobacco auction centers in the country. It was here that the tobacco auction of piles of loose leaves was originated at Neal's Warehouse in the late 1850s. Danville is also the home of the Dan River Mills, the largest single-unit textile mill in the world.

After evacuating Richmond on April 3, 1865, President Jefferson Davis and his cabinet members retreated to Danville, which became the last capital of the Confederacy. While here, Davis wrote his last proclamation as president of the Confederacy, and here he received the news that Lee had surrendered at Appomattox. The town was also made famous when on September 27, 1903, the tragic railroad accident occurred that inspired the folk song, "Wreck of the Old 97." Nancy Witcher Langhorne was born in Danville in 1879. As Lady Astor, she became the first woman member of the British Parliament.

One of the only mechanical grape harvesters in the Northern Hemisphere is used at the Prince Michel Vineyards in Culpepper. The 110-acre winery

Memorial Bridge stands over the Potomac River between Arlington Cemetery and the Lincoln Memorial.

Peaks of Otter on the Blue Ridge Parkway in Bedford County, Virginia.

produces about 150,000 gallons of wine per year, and is known for its award-winning Chardonnay.

Debates grow up throughout the South over whether Virginians are more proud of their ancestors or their ham. Right outside of Jamestown is Smithfield, the ham shrine. The town is close to the island where the Jamestown colonists kept their hogs. According to a law passed in Virginia in 1968, the true Smithfield ham must come from within the corporate limits of Smithfield, be a lean, part-razorback hog, and should be fed a diet of peanuts. It must be cured in salt, and then smoked and processed according to the age-old method. The fine hams produced by this method, but not from Smithfield, are simply called "Virginia Hams."

Virginians have their own geographical place names that can be a trifle confusing. "Southside" stretches from North Carolina to Lynchburg, and refers to the tobacco-growing counties; but it does not include all of the southern area of the state. "Northern

Virginia" is the group of counties related economically to the District of Columbia.

Virginia's majestic Blue Ridge Parkway connects the Shenandoah National Park with the Great Smoky Mountain National Park in North Carolina and Tennessee. The Cumberland Gap National Historical Park was created to honor the historic pass that led settlers through the daunting mountains. The park road closely follows the route taken by Daniel Boone in 1769 and 1775.

The rolling Piedmont Plateau covers nearly half of the state. The Shenandoah Valley and Valley Ridges lie between the Allegheny and Blue Ridge mountains. The 135-mile-long Shenandoah Valley is particularly famous for its apple orchards and its horse country.

Natural Bridge is a magnificent limestone arch which towers two hundred feet over Cedar Creek. It was worshiped by the Monocan Indians as "The Bridge of God." George Washington cut his initials in the bridge when he surveyed it in the eighteenth century. Thomas Jefferson liked it so much that he purchased it from King George III in 1774 for twenty shillings.

The southwestern tip of Virginia is part of the Appalachian Plateau and is made up of ridges and narrow valleys. Bituminous coal from this region is the state's principal product.

In sharp contrast to the green hills and vales of most of the state is the accurately named Dismal Swamp. Lake Drummond is a 3,000-acre swamp of brown water, gnarled cypress trees with tatters of moss, and dense vegetation, giving the area a murky appearance. This unusual lake is even more unusual since it is formed on the side of a hill rather than in a basin.

Close to the hearts of Virginians are the semi- wild Chincoteague ponies thought to have descended from the first horses brought by the English in the 1600s and turned loose off shore on the islands of Chincoteague and Assateague. Each July thousands of spectators still gather to watch the ponies rounded up on the southern end of Assateague Island swim at low tide across the channel to Chincoteague. This seven-mile-long island is connected to the Virginia mainland by bridges on its western shore. The Chincoteague National Wildlife Refuge occupies a third of Assateague Island. It is a refuge for pintail ducks, blue herons, geese, and tundra swans. Assateague Island also includes Assateague Island National Seashore, and it shields Chincoteague from the tides and winds from the sea. The area is known for its shellfish, channel fishing, and goose and duck hunting.

Below: *a roadside stall selling fruit and memorabilia.*

Right: *the lighthouse at Old Point Comfort.*

Above: *Pea Island Wildlife Refuge on Hatteras Island, National Seashore.*
Right: *Pinehurst, in the southern Piedmont, famous for golf
and home to the World Golf Hall of Fame.*

North Carolina

*North Carolina has long been referred to as "the vale of humility between
two mountains of conceit." It has a reputation for being the most progressive and
egalitarian of all of the southern states. North Carolinians must take a special
pride in who they are, since North Carolina has the highest percentage of
native-born residents in the country.*

Many know the state as the headquarters of the
World Methodist Council at Waynesville. Others, as
the site of the PGA World Golf Hall of Fame in
Pinehurst, a resort with seven championship golf
courses. And few missed the recent spectacle of the
fall from grace of TV evangelists, Jim and Tammy Faye
Bakker, and their PTL enterprise in Charlotte.

For decades South Carolina and North Carolina
have argued over Andrew Jackson's birthplace. North
Carolinians swear he was born in Waxhaw, North
Carolina, while he always contended he was born in
South Carolina. North Carolinians reason that he was
only a baby, so how would he have known! Never
mind, the eleventh president of the United States,
James J. Polk, was born and raised in Pineville.
Pepsi-Cola was created in New Bern by pharmacist C.
D. Branham in 1890, and Napoleon's aide Marshall Ney

Above: *a wedding in the North
Carolina Highlands.*

Above: a farm set in the golden fields of eastern North Carolina.

was buried in Cleveland, North Carolina, in the graveyard of the Old Third Creek Presbyterian Church. Legend has it that Ney narrowly escaped execution in France by fleeing to North Carolina. He was buried there in 1846 under the name of Peter Stewart Ney.

North Carolinians take great pride in their award-winning writers. Carl Sandburg, the winner of two Pulitzer Prizes in 1940 and 1951, lived at Connemara, a goat farm in the early community of Flat Rock, from 1945 until his death in 1967. Thomas Wolfe of *Look Homeward, Angel* fame was from Asheville, and William Sydney Porter, O. Henry, was from Greensboro.

North Carolina gained its first notoriety when British explorers returned to England in 1584 with the report that they had discovered a land, "the most plentiful, fruitful and wholesome of all the world." England actually was rather late in joining the race to colonize exotic, untamed lands. Queen Elizabeth and her Golden Age in the late 1500s filled the English with

a passion to "singe the Spaniard's beard," as England was the greatest naval power at that time.

Sir Walter Raleigh, "The Father of British America," came to establish a colony in North Carolina. As a matter of fact, Roanoke Island was the first of Britain's colonies outside of home waters. This first English settlement was established on Roanoke Island in 1585, and it was here that Virginia Dare was the first English child born in America. Unfortunately, the community only lasted a few months. Roanoke was not a good choice for a settlement since it was swampy and low. The settlers had arrived too late to plant; therefore, they soon faced starvation. The Indian population befriended the luckless colonists, and an Indian named Manteo even traveled back to London. He also became the first red man on record to have received baptism in the New World. He became known as "Lord of Roanoke." Today a simple stone marker is all that commemorates the short-lived settlement of Roanoke.

Left: *a child sleeps through a farmers' market in Raleigh.*

Above: *children at the Azalea Festival, Wilmington.*

Raleigh's next colony remains one of the greatest mysteries in United States history. It is known as "The Lost Colony." In 1587 this colony was created on the site of the previous one. Three years later a supply ship arrived and found that the settlement had disappeared. Some contemporary anthropologists have speculated that the 26,000-member Lumbee Indian tribe at Pembroke are descendants of the survivors of this doomed colony.

Carolina was divided into its north and south provinces in 1730. Many of the English settlers had tried Virginia first, but finding that most of the good lands had been sectioned off, moved to North Carolina. A highbrow surveyor, William Byrd, explained the border between North Carolina and his native Virginia in a treatise composed in 1728: "'Tis a thorough aversion to labour that makes people file off to North Carolina, where plenty and a warm sun

65

confirm them in their disposition . . . surely there is no place in the world where the inhabitants live with less labour than in North Carolina.'"

The population swelled as Germans and Scotch-Irish settlers from Pennsylvania and Maryland began to inhabit the back-country. Many highland Scots and English forsook South Carolina for the lake region near Cape Fear.

Wilmington, the state's principal deepwater port, was the scene of the famous Stamp Act resistance in 1765. This rebellious spirit got the attention of the Red Coats. It is believed that the nickname "tar heels" comes from the Revolutionary War Period, when tar was evidently dumped into the rivers to prevent the British from crossing them. When the British waded out of the water, they left tar heel prints wherever they walked.

The Piedmont city of Charlotte was originally named by the settlers to honor Charlotte of Mecklenburg, the queen of King George III of England. Their close ties with the mother country were broken on May 20, 1775, with the Mecklenburg Declaration of Independence. This document is believed to have been the prototype for Thomas Jefferson's document. Later the British General, Lord Cornwallis, referred to Charlotte as a "hornet's nest of rebellion."

In 1789 North Carolina became the twelfth of the original thirteen colonies to join the Union. Raleigh, named for English explorer, Sir Walter Raleigh, was later chosen to be capital because of its central location. When it was founded in 1792, it was

Early morning over the Blue Ridge Mountains near Ashville.

designated as the "the unalterable seat of government."

The Cherokee, one of the most powerful of all American Indian tribes, controlled a large section of the state until the 1830s when many fled the 'Trail of Tears," escaping into the mountains. The Indian population has long been an important component in the state. Today over 8,000 Cherokees live on the largest reservation east of Wisconsin. It covers 50,000 acres in Swain and Jackson Counties, and 13,000 acres in Graham and Cherokee Counties. Their ancient crafts and culture are preserved in the Oconaluftee village in the western mountains.

During the Civil War the non-slave-holding mountain people adamantly opposed slavery; consequently, North Carolina was the next to last state to secede from the Union. The famed Confederate firearm, the Enfield rifle, was manufactured in Asheville.

Strategically North Carolina has long been a valued locale. The first branch of the United States Mint was operated here between 1831 and 1861 and between 1867 and 1913. It was serviced by the one hundred gold mines surrounding Charlotte in the early nineteenth century. Fort Bragg, one of the nation's largest military bases, is located at the head of navigation on the Cape Fear River in Fayetteville, at North Carolina's farthermost inland port. Greenville is the worldwide broadcasting headquarters of the United States Information Agency's *Voice of America.*

The state of North Carolina is approximately two hundred miles from north to south and five hundred miles from east to west, but a great deal of diversity is packed into its small region. To generations of southern children, North Carolina holds memories of a wonderland of mountains cloaked in a smoky blue haze and filled with summer camps, icy mountain streams, and ghost stories about the aberrations of

Facing page: *Cherokee Indian traditional dress worn on the Cherokee Indian Reservation.*

Below: *an off-shore view of Wilmington. The town made its wealth through its port.*

Above: *George Vanderbilt's Biltmore Estate, Ashville, built by Richard Morris Hunt.*

Left: *Biltmore House, the largest private residence in the United States.*

Above: *the Old Well, University of North Carolina, Chapel Hill.*

Right: *a skier in a flurry of snow on Beech Mountain.*

Chimney Rock told around crackling campfires. North Carolina has forty-three peaks that reach more than six thousand feet, giving it an Alpine aspect. Mount Mitchell, rising 6,684 feet, is the highest point east of the Mississippi River. The remoteness of these mountains made them a haven for independent and diverse groups. There are still isolated pockets of inhabitants who speak an Elizabethan dialect that resembles Shakespearian English. In the mountainous region of the state, the majestic Great Smoky Mountains, the master chain of the ancient Appalachian Range, meet the Blue Ridge Mountains. Many geologists claim that the Appalachian chain is over 250 million years old.

The first gold nugget ever found in the United States by white settlers was discovered in 1799 by a twelve-year-old, Conrad Reed, wading in Meadow Creek near Concord. Legend has it that the boy gave the seventeen-pound hunk to his parents to use as a doorstop. In 1802 his father supposedly took the lump of gold to a jeweler in Fayetteville, who bought it for less than $5. Soon North Carolina had the first gold mine in the United States. It was the leading producer of gold in the nation until 1848, when gold was discovered on the western frontier in California.

Rubies and other precious stones have been found near the old Cherokee village of Nikwasi. The town of Franklin is now built around the main Indian mine here.

The mountain resorts of North Carolina have long been popular hideaways for the privileged. For two centuries Asheville has been the most famous mountain resort in the eastern United States. The town is divided by the Swannanoa and French Broad rivers, and is surrounded by the Smokies and Blue Ridge Mountains. Summer residents have included John D. Rockefeller, Thomas Edison, Henry Ford, Grover Cleveland, and Theodore Roosevelt. The resort hotels illustrate various southern resort styles from Georgian Revival to Art Deco.

The largest private residence in the United States was built here in the late nineteenth century by George Washington Vanderbilt, grandson of the railroad magnate Cornelius Vanderbilt. His Biltmore Estate is a 250-room, French Renaissance-style chateau surrounded by 7,500 acres of land. There is a thirty-five acre garden designed by Frederick Law Olmstead, who also planned New York's Central Park. The garden includes a three-thousand-plant rose garden. There is even a working winery.

Today the resort of Blowing Rock is near six winter ski resorts in the Grandfather Mountain/Flat Top area. During Reconstruction, Cashiers became the summer home of the ex-Confederate elite seeking refuge from politics and southern heat. Today it, too, is a popular ski resort.

Forests cover about twenty million acres of the state. At the base of the Blue Ridge Mountains in the central part of North Carolina is the Piedmont region or "foot of the mountains," which covers close to half of the state. It stretches from the foothills to the fall line where the coastal plain begins. The area is both an industrial and educational center. It is bounded by Virginia to the north and South Carolina to the south.

The Moravians settled in this section in Old Salem and Bethabara, and they still practice their faith and customs in an entire mid-eighteenth-century village in Winston-Salem. The original settlement of Winston-Salem dates to 1753 when the Moravian Protestants from Bohemia left the harsh life in Pennsylvania for a new home in North Carolina.

The Sandhills region, known for its longleaf pines and sandy soil, is in the southeastern part of the Piedmont. The climate is dry and cool with brisk winters. The 157,049-acre Croatan National Forest lies the closest to the coast of any national forest in the east. It is home to the pocosin or "swamp on a hill," a soggy sponge-like layer of topsoil on an upland bog. The Venus' flytrap thrives here.

From Rockingham to the Roanoke Rapids, below the fall line, is the coastal plain. The region extends southward from the Virginia border to South Carolina, and stretches eastward to the Outer Banks. Near the 320-mile coastline is a concentration of large lakes. One, Lake Mattamusket, covers approximately thirty thousand acres. The Pamlico and Albemarle Sounds are the largest of the shallow bogs and lagoons that border the coast. They are protected from the seas by

Right: *Great Dismal Swamp, which straddles the border with Virginia.*

Above: *Moravian Old Salem, preserved as a living museum.*

Below: *people tending a Moravian cemetery in Winston-Salem.*

the 150-mile stretch of Outer Banks. These long, narrow barrier islands include Cape Lookout and Cape Hatteras. The Cape Hatteras National Seashore constitutes a forty-five-square-mile length of undeveloped seashore, the most extensive on the Atlantic Coast. Wild ponies still roam along this protected shore. The Cape Hatteras lighthouse, a 208-foot tower constructed in 1870, is the tallest brick structure in the United States.

At Jockey's Ridge State Park on the Outer Banks, there is a 391-square-mile area that once served as the pirate Blackbeard's headquarters. In 1585 this was the site of the first British settlement. The Park also contains the highest natural sand dune on the East Coast. Orville and Wilbur Wright were attracted to this area for their aviation experiments. At Kill Devil Hills, believed to have received its name from rum strong enough to kill, the Wright brothers successfully launched the first flight of a power-driven airplane.

The division between mountain and coastal people is nowhere more striking than in the traditional diet of each. Mountain people of North Carolina have luscious one-pot stews in which all courses are combined. They have their famed poke salad, named because the greens are gathered in a brown paper bag called a "poke." Pokeweed is a wild, pungent green

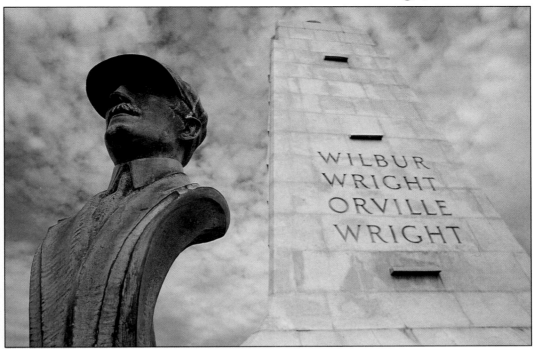

Above: *morning over a beach on Oregon Inlet, Cape Hatteras National Seashore.*

Above right: *the Wright Brothers National Memorial at Kill Devil Hills.*

Right: *hang gliders ride the air from Jockey's Ridge in the mountains of North Carolina.*

native to this region, which is picked in the spring. Settlers learned early that the berries and roots were deadly poison; so only the knowledgeable locals should be trusted to make both a delicious and a safe pot. Another innovation of the mountain diet is their method for doing whole pig barbecues seasoned with red peppers.

Piedmont and coastal diets are more traditionally southern. Crab cakes, however, are to coastal North Carolina what fried chicken is to the Deep South.

Agriculture is still the major component of North Carolina's income, with millions of dollars generated from the production of corn, fruit, peanuts, soybeans, poultry, pulp, and paper. Two-thirds of the nation's brightleaf tobacco is produced here. Durham in the Piedmont section is one of the chief centers in the world for the production of cigarettes and smoking tobaccos. The lively tobacco auctions draw participants from all over the world each fall. While tobacco is North Carolina's chief legal crop, marijuana far exceeds it as the state's principal cash crop.

It was near Durham that William Duke, a poor farmer who had worked in a tobacco factory, began

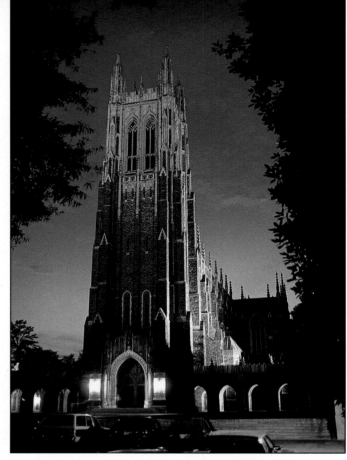

Below: *a herring-processing plant on the Chowan River.*

Right: *the 210-foot bell tower of Duke University's Chapel.*

his modest American Tobacco Company. By 1881 he moved his factory, which processed smoked tobacco, into Durham. Here he introduced a new product, the pre-rolled cigarette. He had perfected the first mechanical process for mass production of cigarettes by 1884. Two of Duke's legacies were the R. J. Reynolds Tobacco Company and Duke University.

The world-famous Research Triangle is a 5,200-acre, wooded center for industrial and governmental research, bounded by the state's three famed institutions, Duke, North Carolina State, and the University of North Carolina. The University of North

Orton Plantation, on the west bank of the Cape Fear River, was built for "King" Roger Moore by about 1735.

Carolina at Chapel Hill is also noted as the nation's oldest state university, having opened on January 15, 1795.

Of all the southeastern states, North Carolina ranks first in manufactured goods. Fieldcrest Cannon, Burlington, and Hanes are just three of the world's most famous textile mills located in the state. It is estimated that one-half of the nation's stockings are made in the Piedmont area around Winston-Salem.

Above: *Abraham Lincoln Birthplace National Historic Site near Hodgenville.*
Right: *Kentucky's rolling hills dotted with homesteads
and trees darned with the colors of fall.*

Kentucky

*The Bluegrass State is made up of a group of diverse regions as varied as
its native sons: Colonel Harland Sanders of Kentucky-Fried-Chicken fame; Cassius
Marcellus Clay, the nineteenth-century abolitionist and ambassador to Russia;
and his twentieth-century namesake, fighter Cassius Clay, who later became
Muhammed Ali.*

Both Civil War presidents were born here one
year apart and one hundred miles distant. Abraham
Lincoln, the sixteenth president of the United States,
was born at Sinking Spring Farm, near the south fork
of the Nolin River, three miles south of Hodgenville,
Kentucky, on February 12, 1809. The Confederacy's
only president, Jefferson Davis, was born at Fairview,
Kentucky. Today there is a 351-foot obelisk, one of the
largest monuments in the United States, erected by
the Daughters of the Confederacy in 1924, to
commemorate the event. Davis's birthday, June 3,
1808, is still a state holiday in five of the former
Confederate states.

Stephen Foster's song, "My Old Kentucky Home,"
sentimentalizes the serenity of the state, while Samuel
Clemens extols Fulton County's beauty in his *Life on
the Mississippi*. In the family of southern states,

Above: *the Jefferson Davis
Monument near Hopkinsville.*

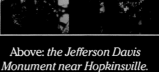

Left: *a barge on a Kentucky river, used to transport coal and tobacco.*

Above: *coal mining, a major industry in the Appalachian region of Kentucky.*

Kentucky is perhaps the wise old grandpa. It lies between the Appalachian Range and the Mississippi River, with the Ohio River forming an irregular northern border. The state boasts of more miles of running water than any other state in the Union except Alaska. There are narrow, deep purple valleys and breathtaking gorges intersecting a maze of ridges.

Approximately three thousand caves honeycomb Kentucky, including Mammoth Cave, the largest explored system in the world. The tallest dome is 192 feet high; the deepest pit is 105 feet deep; and the temperature rarely gets higher than sixty degrees. It is said to contain over eight hundred miles of passageways on five levels. It is believed that the cave was inhabited from 2,500 B.C. until the time of Christ's birth. During the War of 1812, Mammoth Cave

furnished enough saltpeter to make 400,000 pounds of gunpowder.

The most famous safe in the world is located at Fort Knox, Kentucky. At different times this bombproof container has been used to protect the Magna Carta, the British Crown Jewels, the United States Constitution, and the Declaration of Independence. The one-hundred-foot-square receptacle was completed in 1937 and, with its granite facing, holds a large portion of the United States' gold reserve.

Geographically the Appalachian Mountains are the world's oldest mountains. Located in the eastern part of Kentucky, this rugged region includes close to one-third of the land, but a small percentage of the population. Coal mining began on a large scale in 1876 in the foothill country around Harlan County.

Daniel Boone traversed what is now twenty-one counties of the region. Today the 666,000-acre Daniel

79

Boone National Forest encompasses the entire eastern area of Kentucky. It includes the magnificent high, sandstone Red River Gorge, which is made up of over fifty natural arches. Sky Bridge is a ninety-foot stone span, while Natural Bridge has an opening that is sixty-five feet wide and over eighty feet tall.

The Jackson Purchase area is in the southwestern-most portion of the state. Its fertile farmlands and plains gently slope towards the Mississippi River. The last part of the state to be settled, it has been significantly altered by the Tennessee Valley Authority's 170,000-acre, wooded peninsula between Lake Barkley and Lake Kentucky. This is one of the greatest bird migration routes in America. A sulfur springs and ancient salt lick littered with prehistoric mammal bones were discovered in this region by French explorer Charles Le Moyne in 1729.

The fertile bluegrass area west of the Appalachians and south of the Ohio River was the favorite destination of Kentucky's settlers after the discovery of the Cumberland Gap, an old animal and Indian

Above: *Abraham Lincoln, Hodgenville's most famous citizen.*

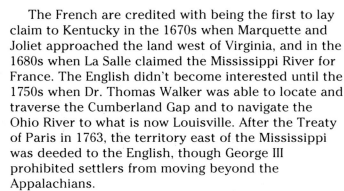

passage, in 1750. They were enchanted by the blue wild flowers that blanketed the countryside in May. It was here that a thriving, slave holding, plantation society grew up. Washington, incorporated in 1786, boasts of being the first town in America named for George Washington. It was an active settlement on the Buffalo Trace, with many of the houses dating to the eighteenth century.

It is from the bluegrass region that the famed style of American music which bears its name was born. Danville, Kentucky, a city founded in 1775 as the official seat of the Virginia government west of the Allegheny Mountains, is considered the official birthplace. The inspiration for the music, however, is purely from the poor, white, primarily Scotch-Irish settlers who lived in the isolated regions of Appalachia. This traditional version of country music wasn't introduced on the stage of the Grand Ole Opry in Nashville until just before World War II. It features singers accompanied by non-electrified string instruments such as banjos, fiddles, and guitars.

The French are credited with being the first to lay claim to Kentucky in the 1670s when Marquette and Joliet approached the land west of Virginia, and in the 1680s when La Salle claimed the Mississippi River for France. The English didn't become interested until the 1750s when Dr. Thomas Walker was able to locate and traverse the Cumberland Gap and to navigate the Ohio River to what is now Louisville. After the Treaty of Paris in 1763, the territory east of the Mississippi was deeded to the English, though George III prohibited settlers from moving beyond the Appalachians.

This, of course, was an open invitation for the brave at heart and free of spirit. Daniel Boone and his brother Squire, John Finley, and James Harrod were among the many who rose to the challenge, with Harrod founding the town of Harrodsburg in 1775 for Virginia. It became the oldest permanent English settlement west of the Allegheny Mountains. Two centuries later the community was to become famous for another achievement. The Shakers, a religious group named for the dance they performed as part of their ritual, made an outstanding contribution to Kentucky cuisine. In 1807 this group formed a community near Harrodsburg, where men and women lived on separate sides of the same buildings and practiced celibacy. They did, however, love good food. One of their greatest contributions to the cuisine of the South is the tart lemon pie.

Left: a farm nestled in Kentucky's mist-shrouded, autumnal hills.

Below: Kentucky's much-loved Bluegrass music.

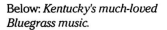

Above: *Daniel Boone's cabin near Carlisle, built in 1795.*

Eventually Kentucky was established as a large Virginia county. Settlers poured in, and by 1784 there were thirty thousand inhabitants. It was a haven for dissatisfied frontiersmen, who disliked the stratified economic and social structures of Virginia and South Carolina.

Once in the Kentucky lands, these settlers continued to be at odds with the government in Virginia. By 1790 the separatists in Kentucky had petitioned the United States Congress for an admittance to the Union as the nation's fifteenth state, the first one on the western frontier. Its political center was established at Frankfort in 1792 when that town was chosen as a compromise capital between factions who wanted either Louisville or Lexington. It was here that Daniel and Rebecca Boone were buried.

Frankfort is in the heart of the tobacco and whiskey country. It is noted for its exquisite capitol building, constructed in 1910 of Indiana limestone and Vermont granite. The rotunda and dome were copied from the Hôtel des Invalides, which houses Napoleon's tomb in Paris, and the state reception

Below: *Boone Trace, Kentucky.*

Right: *a watermill in Kentucky woodlands.*

Left: *the Governor's Mansion, Frankfort, modeled on Marie Antoinette's Petit Trianon.*

Above: *the Kentucky State Capitol and Governor's Mansion, Frankfort.*

room was designed in the style of Louis XV. The fireplaces are exact replicas of those in Marie Antoinette's Salon of Diane in the Palace of Versailles. The governor's mansion was built in 1914. It sits on a bluff overlooking the Kentucky River and was built after the style of the Petit Trianon at Versailles.

Because Kentucky was a slave state that never seceded from the Union, there are many residents of the Deep South who will scoff that Kentuckians are really Yankees. They like to ignore the fact that Bowling Green seceded from the rest of the state, elected its own governor, and was the thirteenth star in the Confederate flag. Never mind, Kentucky has several arguments as to its "southernness," not the least of which is bourbon! Bourbon is a serious matter to a southerner. Just try to hint that a mint julep is as good when made with rum, and hope that there isn't a loaded firearm handy.

Georgetown, Kentucky, is noted as the birthplace of bourbon. The town, named for George Washington, was originally located in the French settlement in Bourbon County, Virginia. When Kentucky split off from Virginia, Bourbon County was part of the new territory. A Baptist minister, Reverend Elijah Craig, is credited with inventing the brew from which bourbon was born in 1789. It is believed that when Baptist Georgetown College was constructed in 1840, a quart of Reverend Craig's recipe was placed under each of the six Ionic columns that support the portico.

Each Kentucky distillery has its own secret formula prepared by cooling a mash of corn, wheat, or rye and barley malt in pure, iron-free water from Kentucky

Above: *an attractive bourbon-processing plant.*

Right: *the raw ingredients of Bourbon: malt, rye, and at least 51% corn.*

limestone springs. By law, all bourbon must be at least fifty-one percent corn. Once distilled, the liquor is aged in charred, white-oak barrels to impart bourbon's distinctive amber color and mellow flavor. Law also requires that bourbon be aged at least two years. Hard-core bourbon drinkers argue that the world's mellowest brews are distilled in the areas around Bardstown, Frankfort, Lawrenceburg, Louisville, and Loretta.

Roughly two-thirds of the country's burley tobacco is grown in western Kentucky. The tobacco auctioneer's chant has long been the theme of Hopkinsville – one of the leading tobacco sales markets in the nation. The town is also known for its production of bowling balls.

The famed twelve-hundred-square-mile thoroughbred area is located in the Bluegrass Country. Since 1875 the Kentucky Derby at Churchill Downs in Louisville is where such thoroughbreds as Man O'War, Whirlaway, Secretariat, and Seattle Slew have thundered to glory on the first Saturday in May at the "Run for the Roses." It is the oldest continuously-held horse race in the country.

Louisville (pronounced Loo-uh-vul) was named

Facing page: *a gracious home near Bowling Green.*

Above: *the evening skyline of Louisville on the Ohio River.*

after Louis XVI in appreciation for his help to America during the American Revolution. Strategically located on a plain adjacent to the Falls of the Ohio River, the city has long been an important post of the New Orleans commercial empire. It became a popular settlement among wealthy Louisiana Creole families and prosperous German food brokers. Today it is Kentucky's largest city, and it has a world-famous symphony and repertory theater. Its industries include the Philip Morris Company, whiskey, horses, and electrical appliances.

Churchill Downs is not the only race course in Kentucky. Lexington, the second largest city in the state, has the Keeneland Race Course, where the pre-Derby Bluegrass Stakes are held, and the Red-Mile Track, the oldest harness track in Kentucky. The Lexington Jockey Club was the first ever organized in the country.

Lexington is the commercial heart of the Bluegrass. It maintains all of the grace of the refined nineteenth-century southern town, while serving as home for over fifty major industries and as one of the South's chief agri-business centers. The lands around the city produce most of the air-cured, dark tobacco used for chewing and close to ninety percent of the dark-fired

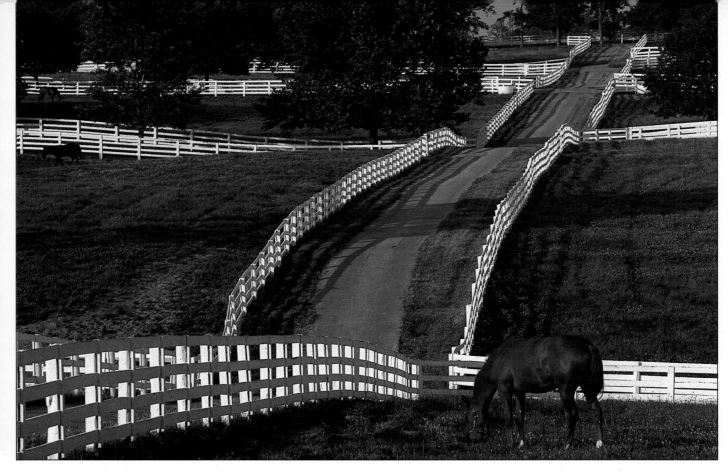

Above: *the fields and white fences of Tom Gentry Farm.*

Left: *the milling crowds at Derby Day spill over Churchill Downs, Louisville.*

Below: *the Kentucky Derby, Churchill Downs, Louisville.*

leaf tobacco used for snuff. It is estimated that over 100 million pounds of tobacco are sold in its market, the largest loose-leaf tobacco market in the world.

It also is the home of the oldest institution of higher learning west of the Allegheny Mountains, Transylvania University. Jefferson Davis was one of its graduates, as were fifty United States senators, thirty-six governors, and two United States vice presidents.

Above: *state highways, offering an advertising opportunity not to be missed.*
Right: *a valley in the Blue Ridge Mountains of Tennessee.*

Tennessee

Tennessee is a state of deep-rooted values, contrast, and an element of surprise. Not the least of these surprises is the fact that the state gem is the pearl, which was taken from mussels in the state's freshwater rivers.

History and terrain, hardship and kinship have combined to create a people alive with character, legend, and song. The land is full of contradictions – risk and security, abundance and loneliness. It is said that outside of every courthouse in rural Tennessee is a Liar's Bench, a place where yarn-spinners, lawyers, historians, and preachers gather to dazzle one another with their tales. From the blues of the lowland cotton country to the bluegrass and country ballads of the coal-producing mountains, Tennessee spreads its soul to the world. Religious fundamentalism runs deep. H. L. Mencken once said of religion in Tennessee: "They do not profess it; they believe in it."

As Tennessee is the border between the east and the west, it is no accident that the first president to challenge the political leadership of New England and Virginia should come from Tennessee. Native son

Above: *Columbia, founded in 1807 on the Duck River.*

The Hermitage, one-time Nashville home of Andrew Jackson. Jefferson Davis called it "a roomy log house."

Andrew Jackson, became the standard-bearer of the United States from 1824 to 1840. He rose from relative obscurity to become a Nashville lawyer, a national war hero, and a champion of the common man. Jackson is credited with several accomplishments. As the seventeenth president of the United States, he restructured the American political system and office of the presidency. The Trail of Tears was also his handiwork, in which fourteen thousand Cherokee Indians were forced to leave their homeland and were marched to Oklahoma. One-quarter of them were to die en route.

Davy Crockett was another famed native son who personifies the spirit of the American West. He was not actually born on a mountaintop, but by picturesque Limestone Creek in Greene County on August 17, 1786. His biographers say that he could be as elegant a dandy as any elder statesman of the day when he didn't feel up to the buckskins and coonskin cap. He took a heroic stand against Andrew Jackson's brutal plan to remove the Cherokees from their homeland. After he voted against the plan, he lost his seat in Congress. Thereupon, he told his Tennessee constituents to "take a long walk off a short pier," and off he went to Texas.

It was in Tennessee that in April of 1877 Adolph S. Ochs started *The Chattanooga Times*, which he later expanded to New York where his *New York Times* still thrives. The famous Scopes Trial, in which the theory of evolution was debated, took place in Dayton in 1925. In 1942 thousands of Ph.D's quietly arrived at Oak Ridge, where they produced Uranium 235 for the first atomic bomb.

Tennessee has attracted a variety of idealists. Hernando de Soto and his band of weary Spaniards hauled their heavy armor and squealing hogs to western Tennessee in their arduous quest for gold. It was here that de Soto died. And here, too, was where the life of Dr. Martin Luther King, Jr., Nobel Prize winning advocate of non-violent civil rights agitation, was to end. He had gone to Memphis in 1968 to help settle a garbage strike when a gunman shot him outside his motel room. Rugby, Tennessee, owes its origins and mystique to Thomas Hughes, English social reformer and author of *Tom Brown's Schooldays*. He named the utopian community for his boyhood school in England. To break with English tradition, he

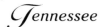

wanted it to be a haven for the second sons of the aristocracy. Unfortunately this post-Civil-War town followed his beliefs only until harsh winters and political mismanagement toppled the idealistic regime and opened the door for small-town American political practices.

The University of the South was established in 1857 in the town of Sewanee, and is governed by twenty-eight Episcopal dioceses in twelve states. Its ethereal campus is located on ten thousand acres of forests, lakes, and bluffs.

Four decades before the Emancipation Proclamation, the first anti-slavery journal came from Jonesboro, the oldest town in Tennessee. The monthly, *The Emancipator*, and its forerunner, *The Manumission Intelligence*, were read throughout the country. Today Jonesboro boasts the nation's oldest and largest storytelling festival. And on the Cumberland Plateau, the city of Free Hill was created before the Civil War as a totally black community. Yet it was in Pulaski during Reconstruction that the first klavern of the Ku Klux Klan had its birth. Tennessee is also the home of *Roots* author, Alex Haley. He grew up in Henning, and has recently moved back to his home state, purchasing a farm in Norris. The town is noted for its famed Museum of Appalachia, which honors life on the frontier.

Below: *the University of the South, Sewanee.*　　**Right:** *Minnie Pearl and Roy Acuff at the Grand Ole Op'ry.*

Tennessee has been called the Musical Garden of Eden of America. Percolating deep in the remote mountains and hill country of Tennessee was a music born of frustration, isolation, and passion for the settlers' homeland.

The blues singers of West Tennessee molded their spirituals and field chants on an ancient tradition of African motifs. In the East Tennessee hill country, settlers drew on their balladic musical traditions to create country music. Folklorists and anthropologists find remnants of Elizabethan English and a folk music with roots in Scottish Highland ballads and Irish folk music dating as far back as the sixteenth century.

These balladeers and guitar pickers had little or no contact with the black culture which produced the blues until well after Reconstruction. Between 1871 and the turn of the century, freed blacks and these isolated whites came together to protest the woes of the mine workers. It is believed that this situation inspired Charles Bowman's song, "Nine-Pound Hammer." Here he combined the chants of the black railroad workers with the country laments from the hills.

By 1900 the term "hillbilly" had come into usage in the Eastern press. With the advent of radio in the 1920s, Tennessee became the crucible of American music. On October 28, 1925, Nashville's WSM Barn Dance made its debut on radio. The name was soon changed to "The Grand Ole Opry." It became the longest-running radio program in American history. Each Saturday night generations of southerners gathered around their radios to hear the live broadcast of their favorite performers. By 1927 RCA had recorded the Carter family and Jimmie Rodgers to satisfy their eager fans.

Hank Williams, Elvis Presley, and Tennessee Ernie Ford were just a few of the performers who were launched by the Opry. From Tennessee came the first

Above: *Grand Ole Op'ry radio show, Opryland, Nashville.*

television musicians who went on the air to sing the praises of such products as Martha White flour. In the 1960s and 1970s followed the "Beverly Hillbillies."

Tennessee had its origins in the overmountain region of colonial North Carolina, a vast territory of 42,244 square miles. It was known as North Carolina's "western lands." From the beginning, though, Tennessee was different from the other colonies. Its name came from a native river, not English royalty. The land is wedged between the North and the South, the established East and the western frontier. Called the "Land of Western Waters," its rivers drain south to the Gulf rather than east to the Atlantic. Situated at the exact center of the eastern United States, over half of the land is covered by forests. Throughout its history, its land and rivers have captivated and molded the legends and beliefs of its inhabitants.

The buffalo were the first engineers of this frontier. Their hooves trampled the first paths, which the Indians then expanded. These early wilderness trails

became a loosely connected system of paths, followed by the first explorers and pioneers, which led from the Potomac River to the Falls of Ohio. Daniel Boone and his thirty axmen traversed this rugged trail, opening a path for 300,000 pioneers to follow into Tennessee from 1775 to 1800. Later the road served as the artery that brought Union and Confederate troops into the bloody battles of the Civil War.

Long before de Soto visited the site of Memphis in 1540, Tennessee was civilized. From their capital near what is now Cleveland, Tennessee, the Cherokee dominated the state, as well as parts of Georgia and the Carolinas. Even before the civilizations in the Euphrates Valley, the archaic Indians had roamed the woods and caves clothed in animal skins. Archeologists have found indications that these Indians had the richest culture of any native people north of Mexico. For thousands of years the Indians had believed in a system of relationships within a natural cycle so that each could serve the other –

Left: *tumbling water flowing through Fall Creek Falls State Resort Park.*

Above: *Knoxville, named for General Henry Knox, Washington's Secretary of War.*

plants fed animals which fed humans who fed plants. Yet within a few generations, the white man imposed a new philosophy triumphant over nature: conquest.

In order to get settlers to move to the western frontier, war veterans were paid in land in the Cumberland Valley. English, Irish, Scots, Swiss, Poles, Germans, French Huguenots, and people from North Carolina, South Carolina, Virginia, and Pennsylvania sought a new start here. West Tennessee soon proved to be a profitable region for growing tobacco and, later, cotton; consequently large numbers of slaves were brought in.

Tennessee is a rough parallelogram. It is approximately 432 miles from east to west and 120 miles from north to south. Some of the tallest mountains in the eastern United States bracket one side, while the largest river in North America helps to shape the other. It has been said that these dual features exemplify the powerful forces that set Tennessee apart – the mountains lock in the soul, while the rivers flow out with the spirit.

After North Carolina offered to cede its western land to the United States in 1784, the Watauga settlers, angry at its transfer without consent, established the new state of Franklin. Although the state was never recognized by Congress, Franklin endured for four years, electing officials, creating laws, and collecting taxes.

In 1792 Knoxville became the capital of the territory. Governor William Blount built a clapboard mansion with windows, called by local Indians "the house with many glass eyes." By 1796 the population had increased to sixty-seven thousand, which allowed Tennessee to qualify for statehood. It became the sixteenth state, only the second west of the Appalachians. Soon it was to earn its nickname, the "Volunteer State." In the Mexican War, Tennessee was asked to supply twenty-eight hundred soldiers; thirty thousand men volunteered to fight alongside Andrew Jackson.

By the Civil War Tennessee was the fifth most

populous state in the Union. The valley farmlands around Knoxville made it the greatest corn-producing state, winning it the nickname of the "Hog and Hominy State." While it was basically anti-slavery, Lincoln's official call for troops changed its allegiance to the Confederate side. Philosophically, the sentiments of the people were split, making for the tragic reality of brothers fighting brothers and sons fighting fathers. On June 8, 1861, Tennessee seceded from the Union, making it one of the last states to do so. Tennessee soldiers, numbering 115,000, fought for the Confederacy, while 31,000 joined the Union forces. It became the first former Confederate state to rejoin the Union when the conflict was over. And Nashville became its capital.

Two of the War's greatest leaders came from the state, though they fought on opposing sides. Admiral David Glasgow Farragut of Knoxville commanded the Union naval forces at Vicksburg, and, thirteen months later, led the Union squadron to victory in the Battle of Mobile Bay. On the Confederate side, Nathan Bedfor Forrest attained lasting fame through brilliant and

Knoxville fire company, ready for action.

effective use of cavalry.

By the Great Depression, parts of Tennessee were looked on more as a Third World country than as part of the United States. The one great state resource that seemed a natural solution was the Tennessee River. The Tennessee Valley trisects the state in a lazy oxbow before finally joining up with the Ohio River. Its natural configuration made it ideal as a producer of hydroelectricity.

On May 18, 1933, President Franklin D. Roosevelt signed the Tennessee Valley Authority Act (TVA), which developed an unprecedented system of navigation, flood control, and power generation for a seven-state area. With its headquarters in Knoxville, the TVA consolidated Tennessee, Alabama, Georgia, Kentucky, Mississippi, North Carolina, and Virginia into a service area roughly the size of Great Britain. It transformed the natural watershed into one hundred miles of waterways, flood control, and a stairway of locks, dams, and lakes which would provide power to seven million people. Some saw the TVA, America's largest federally-owned utility, as "Big Brother," while others saw it as the last hope to vitalize one of the most poverty-stricken sections of the nation by improving existing roads, building highways and school systems, and by providing employment and job training to thousands. The Thirty Great Lakes of the South were created, and in conjunction the TVA developed 139 recreational areas. Some of these are game preserves where endangered bald eagles and buffalo now abound.

A nineteenth-century governor explained: "Tennessee lies in the happiest lines of longitude and latitude; she lies on the dividing line between the two great agricultural regions of the world. To the South are tropical fruits, flowers and cotton and to the North are apples and cereal grains. Here pecans of the South fall among the hickory nuts of the North. The magnolia blooms in the same grove where the apple ripens."

Tennessee has been called the "three regions," producing a people of dogged regionalism. To the east, Tennessee's land touches the horizon. It is landlocked by the Great Smokies, the Unakas, and the Cumberlands. Closer geographically to the Great Lakes than to the Gulf of Mexico, old men in the village of Moss still play an ancient marble game called rolley hole. Set beside the tennis courts and pools are well-groomed rolley hole yards. Here is a green quiet world, opulent with stands of oak, hickory, poplar, ash, locust, walnut, and maple trees. There are mosses and ferns, waxy green galax, and hillsides splashed with dogwood and the Catawba rhododendron. The magnificent rhododendron is a member of the heath family, a relative of Scottish heather. Its gnarled trunk can be up to fifteen feet tall

Above: *the Tennessee River Dam.*

Right: *Opryland Themepark, Nashville.*

and can support over seven hundred blossoms. The name comes from the Greek "rhodon" or rose, and "dendron" for tree.

Geologists reckon the age of the Ocoee series of rocks that prevails in the Great Smokies to be more than 500 to 600 million years old. They are so old, in fact, that in some places there are neither plant nor animal fossils. When prehistoric glaciers moved across North America, the mass of ice did not cover the Great Smokies; thus a variety of plants grown here became the seedbed for states to the north once the earth began to warm.

The spine of the ancient Great Smoky Mountains runs astride the border for seventy miles between northeastern Tennessee and northwestern North Carolina. The name comes from the Indians who called these mountains "The Land of Smoke." There are sixteen peaks that are over 6,000 feet high. Roan Mountain, at 6,286 feet, dominates its immediate surroundings by 4,000 feet. A unique feature is the six miles of luxuriant rolling meadows on its summit called "balds." Each June these meadows become a

97

wonderland of pink, rose, and lavender rhododendrons.

The mountainous east is hickory-smoked Appalachia. Here is a breed of down-home conservative Republicans. It is an area known for backwoods moonshiners. It took the high price of sugar in the 1970s to do what the Feds could never do – put these men out of business. Today many remote woodsmen have replaced one contraband with another, and they grow marijuana in their hidden backwoods fiefdoms.

Gatlinburg stands at the gateway to the Great Smoky Mountains National Park. In the winter it is the most geographically southern of ski resorts, while in summer it is a boom town for vacationers on their way to America's most visited park.

The Great Smoky Mountains National Park was created in 1934. It consists of eight hundred square miles with two hundred thousand acres of virgin hardwood, one of the largest forests in North America. There are about fifty thousand acres of red spruce, many of which are over four hundred years old. Here birds migrate vertically, seeking the cool spruce-covered highlands in summer and the moderate valley in winter. The area is home to fifty types of animals and eighty types of fish.

Chattanooga is one of the largest of the famed valley cities of Tennessee. From Lookout Mountain on a clear day, visitors can see seven states. The city was one of the places where Union soldiers resettled with their families after the Civil War. Due to its strategic location on the railroad, it became a burgeoning industrial center by the end of Reconstruction. Today the Chattanooga Choo-Choo Hilton keeps the elegance of the nineteenth century alive, quartering guests in railroad parlor cars of the last century at the old railroad yard.

Anyone who has ever traveled through the South by automobile has seen signs plastered on sides of barns, painted on boulders, screaming from billboards: "See Rock City." Like the Grand Canyon and Coney Island all rolled up into one, this is a ten-acre "city" near Chattanooga made of rare, lichen-covered sandstone. The four-thousand-foot-long Enchanted Trail leads through tunnels of various heights and down through narrow crevices, and a suspension bridge spans beautiful chasms. Ruby Falls must be reached by an elevator, for the 145-foot falls are over 1,000 feet underground. The Incline Railway has thrilled generations of funseekers.

Next to the ancient geological formations are some relatively new areas. From December 16, 1811, to March 15, 1812, northwestern Tennessee was shaken by earthquakes that tumbled land, trees, and streams and filled the air with the stench of sulfur. Many felt the Day of Judgment had arrived. Trees were

uprooted by the thousands, bluffs were obliterated by landslides, the earth sank, and the Mississippi River reversed its course and surged north. Reelfoot Lake, a twenty-five-thousand-acre mystical world of cypress trees, was formed when these New Madrid earthquakes rattled the Mississippi River Valley. By 1920 a levee had been built to keep the river from overrunning the area's farmland. A spillway was added in 1931 to maintain a constant level, which is causing the Reelfoot to stagnate.

Middle Tennessee is the second great region of Tennessee. It is characterized by big business and moderate politics. Here the slow roll of white rail fences bespeaks old money, horse farms, and security. Three American presidents have lived in this region. The limestone that underlies much of this part of the state is the source of the filtered water for the famed Tennessee whiskey from the Jack Daniel Distillery in Lynchburg.

The central location makes it an ideal financial and industrial hub. General Motors recently chose the tiny community of Spring Hill as the site of its Saturn auto factory. It is the biggest single industrial investment in United States history. In addition, nearly ten percent of all Japanese investments are located in this region

Above: *morning mist swirls around a farm in Tennessee.*

Right: *Vanderbilt University, Nashville.*

of Tennessee. The $745-million Nissan plant has been operating here since 1983.

Technically to be called a Tennessee walking horse, the animal must be raised and trained on one of twenty-five farms within a four-mile radius of Shelbyville. This famed home-grown breed is exceedingly popular with eastern horse gentry. The horse business was the catalyst for pulling middle Tennessee out of the Depression.

Nashville, the financial and cultural center of this area, began as a cluster of log cabins in the late eighteenth century. By the time of the Civil War, it had grown to be the eighth largest city in the South and an important commercial center for both steamboats and railroads.

It was called the "Athens of the West," a citadel of culture and education on the frontier. Later this title was changed to the "Athens of the South." For the Centennial of 1897, a full-sized replica of the Parthenon was constructed. This caused several nonplussed "good ole boys" to comment, "Don't they

realize that this was only called Athens 'cause it is eighty-five miles up the road from Sparta!" Others reason that there must be some connection with Greece and ancient Rome since two of the most popular male names in the region are Homer and Virgil.

By the Civil War, Nashville was noted both for its educational institutions and its large printing industry. Religious books, especially the Bible, were produced at an unprecedented rate. Today there are over seven hundred churches in the city. It is also the headquarters of the powerful Southern Baptist Association and a stronghold of fundamentalism, earning Nashville the nicknames "Buckle of the Bible Belt" and "Protestant Vatican."

Today there are fifteen educational institutions, which include Vanderbilt University; Fisk, one of the first private black colleges in the South; and Meharry Medical College, the first black medical school in the United States.

"The Wall Street of the South" is yet another of

Ryman Auditorium, the original Grand Ole Opryhouse.

Nashville's identities. It is a center of insurance and banking corporations. A variety of small businesses that began in Nashville and have become world-renowned include Maxwell House Coffee, Jack Daniel Whiskey, Winn-Dixie, Stokely Van Camp, Ingram Book Company, and Holiday Inns.

The society that goes along with these financial empires rivals Palm Beach for sophistication. Stately mansions line the streets of Belle Meade, one of the South's most prestigious addresses. Each year the Swan Ball to benefit one of the museum homes, Cheekwood, is one of the grandest and most profitable fund-raisers in America. In the surrounding Williamson County, the society anglophiles don red jackets and chase foxes cross-country. It is one of the few places in America that Princess Anne regularly comes to ride.

Just a few miles down the road from Belle Meade, but continents away culturally, is the Nashville that the rest of the world knows and loves – "The Country Music Capital of the World," "The Third Coast," "Music City USA." Over two hundred music publishing firms and record companies, agents, and producers are packed into a fourteen-block district called Music Row. More than one-half of all single records produced in the United States come out of Nashville. It is the home of ninety percent of all country music stars because of the fact that their principal audience lives in a six-hundred-mile radius of Nashville. Today Nashville's country music station, WSM radio, still has the tallest radio tower in America, though the Grand Ole Opry no longer performs in the old Ryman Auditorium. Opryland USA is fourteen miles upriver, part of a mega-entertainment and convention facility.

Four hundred fifty miles to the west, on the plateau of the Mississippi River, the Tennessee horizon is level. River bluffs overlook fertile fields of cotton and soybeans.

West Tennessee is the third region of Tennessee. It is the Deep South – democratic, agricultural, and a stronghold of low-country genteel values. Its principal city is Memphis. In 1819 Andrew Jackson helped found and name a new settlement on the Mississippi in the new territory of Tennessee. He was evidently inspired by the Nile-like illusion of the location; thus the founder called the town Memphis, meaning "a place of good abode." With the advent of cotton, it became the unofficial Delta capital, the urban center for a two-hundred-mile radius of rural plantations in Mississippi, Arkansas, and Missouri. It was soon the largest slave market in the Central South and the largest inland cotton market in the South.

Reconstruction brought a disastrous period to the city. What few fortunes survived the Civil War were destroyed by the financial panic of 1876, and thousands were killed by a yellow fever epidemic. Then in the fall of 1878, another deadly fever struck, which killed twenty-five percent of the city's population. Finally on January 31, 1879, Memphis was forced to declare bankruptcy, and it surrendered its charter to the state of Tennessee. Within five years

Above: *a bust in Belmont Mansion, Nashville.*

Right: *a colorful display at Earl's Fruit Stand in Franklin, an agricultural center.*

Below: *Rattle and Snap Mansion near Columbia, built in 1845 for George W. Polk.*

Above: *the Memphis skyline beyond the Mississippi River.*

Right: *Rhodes College, Memphis.*

the once-prominent cotton brokers and bankers of Memphis had formed a coalition to save the city.

Before the Civil War its Beale Street was the center of aristocratic activity. After the Civil War, as the city's fortunes floundered, so did Beale Street. By the early twentieth century it was the place where rich whites and poor blacks went to gamble and enjoy a variety of vices. Pee Wee's Saloon was one place where people from both sides of the tracks gathered to hear W. C. Handy blow his exotic music called the blues. The music hit it big in 1909 when white political boss, E. H. Crump, asked Handy to write a campaign song for him. The song, "Mr. Crump," is credited with winning the election, and Handy turned the song into "Memphis Blues," the first blues song ever published. In 1977 Congress honored this musical heritage by naming Memphis officially "The Home of the Blues."

For generations the Peabody Hotel has been considered the geographical beginning of the Mississippi Delta, which ends on the Confederate Battlefield of Vicksburg. It is renowned for its traditional duck ritual – twice daily a quartet of ducks marches to and from the lobby fountain, accompanied musically by the robust marches of John Philip Sousa.

Left: *no one can forget that Memphis was the birthplace of the "blues."*

Above: *Graceland, the famous home of Elvis Presley in Memphis.*

During the Civil War the Union army located one of its largest hospitals in Memphis. Today this medical heritage continues. The city boasts the largest number of doctors per capita in the nation, and it has the country's highest percentage of neurosurgeons. It is also the home of the nation's largest private hospital, the Memphis Medical Center, and the St. Jude's Children's Research Hospital, founded by Danny Thomas.

Elvis Presley, the King of Rock and Roll, built his elaborate mansion, Graceland, in Memphis. Each year on August 15, the eve of his death, thousands of fans gather at his home for a solemn vigil accompanied by Elvis's gospel records.

Today Memphis is still a bastion of conservative cotton society and Tennessee's largest city. The port remains one of the most active in the South. It ships more hardwood than any other United States port, and one-third of all of the nation's cotton is brokered in the city. Residents proudly extol its virtues by pointing to recent awards designating Memphis as the country's cleanest city, safest city, and quietest city.

103

Above: *an iris growing wild in Jean Lafitte National Park.*
Right: *fishing boats moored on a bayou near New Oreleans.*

Louisiana

Right from the beginning Louisiana determined to be different from the other southern states. Its name honored France's Louis XIV, a genius and a rake. It is an archipelago of cultures, some vociferously southern, others pugnaciously Creole/Louisiana. The state has been called the Quebec of the United States, yet this definition does not apply to the northern part of the state, which is more akin to Arkansas or Mississippi than to southern Louisiana.

Economically it is its own separate, self-sustaining nation. It ranks first in the production of natural gas, oysters, and crawfish. Strawberries, rice, sweet potatoes, and sugar cane thrive alongside massive petrochemical plants on the banks of rivers. The semitropical climate provides a 330-day growing season. As a result it is said that pine trees and mildew grow faster in Louisiana than anywhere else in the country.

There is a popular misconception that the terms Creole and Cajun are interchangeable, or that all people who live in Louisiana are Cajuns. First of all, the Cajun and Creole populations make up less than half of the people in the state. While there are similarities between the two groups, they have little in common with the Protestant, Anglo-Saxon descendants in the northern part of the state.

Above: *street art in New Orleans' French Quarter.*

The term Creole comes from the Spanish word "criollos," originally denoting persons of European or African descent born outside of their native countries. Later the term came to refer to the sophisticated, worldly urbanites for whom French was the predominant language.

Cajuns, on the other hand, are the provincial country cousins. They were descended from families that had fled religious persecution in France in the early 1500s and had settled in Nova Scotia. In 1755 the British demanded that they pledge allegiance to England or be expelled from Canada. When they refused, they were forcibly rounded up and shipped to the American colonies or back to France. Their history was similar to the Trail of Tears of the Cherokees. Families were split up, and many died on their journey. They spoke an archaic version of French that had not been used for a hundred years. The Spanish government in Louisiana came to their aid by offering them a home in Louisiana.

By 1763 they had begun to found settlements deep in the swamps to the south and west of New Orleans. Life has changed little since then. Their homes are built along lazy, meandering rivers and on lagoons and bayous, teeming with thick grasses, palmettos, and cypress. Air and water are still thick with every type of insect and animal. "Dutch nightingales," frogs, sing a deafening, antiphonal chorus, while alligators and moccasins slither along the banks. Nesting pelicans and slowly flying gulls are joined during the migration seasons by flocks of birds so thick that they cover the sky.

Today these Acadians, called Cajuns, number close to three-quarters of a million, and many still speak a French akin to that of the seventeenth century. Many children in the remote areas gather moss to stuff mattresses, while their fathers still catch alligators by pulling them out of deep holes. Families hunt crabs with "trot lines," baited nets marked by wooden floaters in shallow water, and trappers still go out each foggy morning to trap muskrat and nutria to sell to big-city furriers.

South Louisiana is one of America's truest cultural melting pots, exemplified by its unique cuisine. In a pot of gumbo there is a French roux, African okra, Indian filé powder made from native sassafras, Spanish peppers, Italian-inspired Cajun sausage, and oysters supplied by Yugoslav fishermen. The soup is served over Chinese rice with an accompaniment of hot French bread made by one of Louisiana's fine German bakers and washed down with German-brewed beer.

Louisiana is the original Dixie, named for the

Louisiana State Capitol, Baton Rouge, built in 1932.

French word for ten, "dix," the bills used as legal tender. They were called "dixies" by the Kentucky flatboatmen who traded in New Orleans. Yet the state is distinctly more worldly and exotic than the other southern states. This is even illustrated by its state capitol building, a thirty-four-story building constructed from twenty-six varieties of marble from every marble-producing country in the world.

It has the third longest coastline in the continental United States, which provides both an abundance of seafood and a lucrative offshore oil industry. As the Mississippi meanders to the Gulf, it deposits half-liquid earth in its lengthy advance into the salty blue water, thus creating the vast expanse of Louisiana's fertile deltas. It is one of the flattest states in the Union. The highest point is only about five hundred feet above sea level, and New Orleans is five feet below sea level.

More than forty percent of Louisiana is alluvial land or swamps. The Achafalaya River basin is the United States' last great river-basin swamp of its kind. Within the state there are seventy-five hundred miles of navigable waterways – the Mississippi, the Ouachita, the Red River, and their tributaries meander

Sunset over Atchafalaya Swamp

and salt domes near the Gulf of Mexico. Large tidal bays and lakes dot the landscape, as well as oxbow lakes left when the mighty rivers changed their courses.

In the uplands of the north are areas of low pine hills between the Ouachita and the Red rivers. South of the Red River the land becomes prairie, which blends into a thirty-mile belt of marshland near the coast.

Some of the earliest inhabitants of Louisiana were the Indians at Poverty Point. They were people of the advanced Stone Age, who lived at the site between 1700 and 700 B.C. and are thought to have been the earliest southward movement of the Hopewell culture. Speculation has it that they came either from Asia by way of the Bering Strait or up from Central and South America. Digs indicate that they had iron ore from Arkansas and Mississippi, flint from Ohio, slate from Michigan, and stone from Kentucky and Tennessee.

The Spaniards were the state's first white tourists on record. Some believe that Alvarez de Pineda had discovered the Mississippi River as early as 1519; nevertheless, Hernando de Soto's visit got better publicity. His trip to Louisiana was recorded in 1542. Other Spaniards followed, though none stayed for very long. It would be another hundred years before the white man returned to threaten the bucolic life of native Indians and the wildlife.

In 1682 La Salle and fifty men came down the Mississippi from Canada to claim the entire Mississippi Valley for the French king. The French rule lasted until November 1762 when Louis XV of France, after the French defeat in the Seven Years' War, secretly gave Louisiana to his Spanish cousin, Charles III, in an effort to keep it out of British hands.

For a time the Compagnie des Indes, which originally controlled Louisiana, decided to colonize this deadly marsh with inhabitants of the jails, brothels, and debtors' prisons of France. This policy, when combined with the fact that the French would have starved if it hadn't been for the Indians, created a disastrous situation. Wheat, the staple of the French diet, would not grow in swampy, humid south Louisiana, and the Indian diet of corn was not very palatable to those who survived the first years.

In an effort to recruit farmers to alleviate this situation, the agricultural regions of Germany and Switzerland were inundated with handbills inviting would-be settlers to Louisiana's "paradise." Unfortunately, these farmers didn't take to New Orleans. The large number of German-speaking immigrants in the 1720s quickly tired of "the Paris of the New World," and moved away from the mildew and malaria twenty miles upriver to an area known as the Côte des Allemands. Here they quickly established prosperous farms. With the money they made, many

Germans created large sugar plantations, breweries, bakeries, and banks. After several generations they were back in New Orleans, right in the center of Creole society with Francophile names, and speaking French.

Status quo was not disrupted by the change of administration from French to Spanish. The new Spanish garrison in Louisiana supplied money and provisions to the American Revolutionary forces. They had to smuggle aid past the British fleet to assist George Washington in keeping his American forces together. Morale at Valley Forge was definitely lifted in 1779 when the word came that both the Spanish and French governments had joined the American Revolutionary forces in declaring war on Great Britain.

The Spanish recognized the Mississippi River as the western boundary of the United States, and gave the new nation the right to export products through New Orleans duty free. Soon "Kaintucks" were loading up their flatboats with Monongahela whiskey and heading to New Orleans. These rugged men dressed in buckskins, toting rifles and big dreams, dug in to stay the minute they saw the glamor of the European-style

Left: *the graceful French Quarter of New Orleans.*

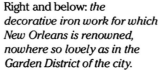

Right and below: *the decorative iron work for which New Orleans is renowned, nowhere so lovely as in the Garden District of the city.*

New World city. Creole society avoided these "barbarians"; as a result, they created their own "American" parts of town.

La Nouvelle Orléans, New Orleans, had been founded in 1718 by the French Canadian Jean-Baptiste Le Moyne, Sieur de Bienville, on a Muskhogean tribal portage at a strategic crescent on the Mississippi River, thirty leagues upriver from the Gulf of Mexico. The actual site was a small, verminous swamp, an area that is marked on maps of the period as inhabited by "savage man-eaters."

By the late eighteenth century New Orleans was one of the most glittering of North American cities. Genteel Creole ladies dressed in the latest Paris fashions, and performances of the latest European operas, ballets, and theater were commonplace. While elegance and style reigned in society, vice and excess in the back streets drew men of all classes, from weary rural plantation owners to flatboatmen, soldiers, and sailors.

The unpleasantness of living in a swamp might be removed from view behind damask and lace, but it was still a factor. As late as a year before the Civil War, ten thousand people died of yellow fever. New Orleans was ravaged by the problems of bubonic plague and flooding. Up until the Civil War wealthy New Orleans businessmen continued the practice of bribing laborers upriver to blow up the levees each spring to divert the swollen Mississippi onto less inhabited sugar country to save the city from flooding. This threat was not eliminated until a massive, late-nineteenth-century drainage system and one of the world's greatest systems of pumps was installed in New Orleans. This was combined with the construction, above New Orleans, of the Bonnet Carre Spillway, a giant safety valve against flooding.

If Atlanta is the pinnacle of the New South, then New Orleans is still its most colorful city. Even Scarlett and Rhett Butler spent their honeymoon in the "Belle City of the South." This lusty, luscious city is credited as the place where the cocktail was invented, where the Mardi Gras spirit reigns supreme from Twelfth Night to Ash Wednesday, and where jazz was created.

The United States made the greatest real estate deal of all times when it bought nine hundred thousand square miles of land for about four cents an acre from France. Spain had secretly retroceded Louisiana to France during Napoleon's reign. The purchase was signed a few days before Christmas in 1803, but it took until 1925 for the two governments to finish up the accounting part. It is estimated that the Americans actually only paid about $12 million. By January 1, 1804, most Louisianians had heard that English was the official language, and that the boisterous "Kaintucks" had every right to call the new territory home.

The transfer of power was not without its problems, however. St. Francisville is one of Louisiana's oldest towns. It was established by Anglo-Saxon settlers on the site of an abandoned Spanish Capuchin monastery. In 1810 it became the capital of the Free and Independent Republic of West Florida, a tiny headstrong nation. This new nation was created when in 1803 the United States purchased a large portion of Louisiana and let their portion of the state revert to Spain. It took years of negotiations to reconnect the state.

Famed naturalist and artist, John James Audubon, came to this community in the early 1800s. For sixty dollars a month, plus room and board, he tutored children, taught dancing, and painted portraits. In his spare time, he hunted, painted birds, and provided comfort to lonely plantation wives.

Political turmoil throughout the world played a crucial part in keeping south Louisiana culturally separate from the other regions of the United States. Aristocrats fleeing the French Revolution added pomp, and those from the West Indies and Santa Domingo

Above: *the milling throngs celebrating Mardi Gras.*

Below: *during Mardi Gras expect the unexpected.*

110 Above: *a family at the Mardi Gras celebrations, New Orleans.*

Right: *an ornate costume worn for Mardi Gras.*

Above: *a statue of Andrew Jackson at the center of New Orleans' Jackson Square.*

Right: *the steamy, atmospheric swamps and waterways for which Louisiana is famous.*

brought with them further techniques for adapting to the climate. Early views of New Orleans show that it was a village quite different from the city of today. The little cottages of the French in the early 1700s were squat, half-timbered structures whose walls were filled with mud mixed with moss and straw. The new settlers from the islands brought with them the idea of the veranda and grander, breezier homes. Later the defeated followers of Napoleon came, many of whom began to prepare to rescue their leader and establish a base for him in Louisiana. Again there was an influx of "state-of-the-art" European culture and style.

The War of 1812 was partially a British attempt to pull the plug on the United States' newfound unity. They reasoned that Louisiana, which had only been an American territory for eight years, would be the most vulnerable spot for attack. They did not, however, foresee the peculiar combination of Creoles, Frenchmen, "Kaintucks," slaves, freed blacks, and pirates that they had to fight.

On Christmas Eve the British had signed a peace treaty with the United States. The word, however, had not reached the troops in Louisiana. The famous Battle of New Orleans took place two weeks later. The defeat of the British by General Andrew Jackson helped to make him a national hero and president of the United States, and it made a legend of his compatriot Jean Lafitte. As a matter of fact, Louisiana is probably the only state in the Union with a national

park named for a pirate.

Jean Lafitte was a native of Santa Domingo who operated a blacksmith shop in the French Quarter as a front for a black-market smuggling operation. Perhaps he was Royal Street's first antiques dealer. He and his band of pirates were such a thorn in the side of the state's governor that the British sought his aid. In 1814 the British gave him a captaincy and thirty thousand dollars in gold. He then attempted to reveal the British plan for the attack to his adversary, Governor Claiborne. Claiborne rewarded Laffite for his support by burning his camp.

Nevertheless, Lafitte and his ruthless pirates aided

Jackson and his Tennessee regiment in the miraculous victory over the same British troops that had defeated Napoleon. A few years after the battle, Lafitte sailed off into the sunset and into the hearts of Louisianians.

Before the Civil War the south Louisianians, having recently seen their area become part of a state, were very pro-Union. In 1856 New Orleanians erected a statue to Henry Clay to honor his attempts to keep the Union together. From January 27 until March 21, 1861, Louisiana stood between the Union and the Confederacy when it formed the Independent Commonwealth of Louisiana. Finally, the passionate southerners of the northern part of the state won out. Yet it was one of south Louisiana's New Orleans Creoles, General Pierre Gustave Toutant de Beauregard, who gave the command for the Confederate attack on Fort Sumter.

New Orleans was the South's largest port, so it was an early target of Union conquest. In April 1862 the city was captured by the Union fleet commander from Tennessee, Admiral David G. Farragut. The federally held portions of Louisiana were the first Confederate territory to be subject to Reconstruction. It began in 1862 when General "Spoons" Butler emancipated the slaves by forcing them to enlist in his Federal regiments. Oddly, Lincoln's Emancipation Proclamation of January 1, 1863, abolished slavery in all southern states, but it was allowed to continue in

Left: *Nottoway, built in 1859 for John Randolph by Henry Howard.*

Below: *a soldier's cap on display in the Confederate War Museum, New Orleans.*

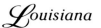

many Union-held areas in Louisiana until the Reconstruction Constitution in 1864.

In many ways Louisiana is a state split down the middle culturally and socially by the Bible Belt in the Celtic fundamentalist north and Le Bon Temps Roule – "Let the Good Times Roll" – of the French-Spanish Catholic regions of the south. Lafayette is the Cajun big city. It is also the home of the National Live Oak Society. The group limits membership to trees that are at least a hundred years old. The membership fee is twenty-five acorns.

South Louisiana is probably the festival and party capital of the world. Almost every town has some to-do to celebrate its most abundant local product. The area is known for its sweet potatoes, the juicy, red tubers erroneously called yams by Yankees. Then there are shrimp, oyster, gumbo, sugar, andouille and boudin sausages, crawfish, and strawberry festivals. Breaux Bridge is the crawfish capital of the world, while one quarter of all rice produced in the United States grows in a sixty-mile radius of Crowley.

Thousands of tourists annually travel the back roads of South Louisiana, seeking glimpses of this unique culture. One of the favorite spots is the

Evangeline Oak, made famous by the Henry Wadsworth Longfellow poem. It was here that Evangeline and her lover were supposed to have met.

Zydeco, dixieland, ragtime, bee-bop, and jazz also emerged from the African-American culture of south Louisiana near New Orleans. The plaintive wailing of trombones at funerals merged with the hot notes of ragtime to form jazz, while the rinky-tinky of the French Cajun music combined with these same African rhythms to create zydeco.

The early citified ragtime bands were called "spasm" bands. They played improvised music in the area known as Storyville, the colorful section of New Orleans known for honky-tonks, gambling clubs, and bordellos. Instruments, too, were improvised – a bass fiddle could be made of a barrel, a soapbox could be the basis for a guitar. These exotic, stirring rhythms simmered in the back streets of New Orleans until right before World War I, when talent scouts took Dixieland to the clubs of Chicago and New York.

Today the New Orleans Jazz and Heritage Festival, held the first two weekends in May, is the largest music festival in the world. An average of sixty thousand people a day come from far and wide to hear eleven stages of continuous jazz-inspired music from noon to dark.

Below: *jazz musicians performing in New Orleans' Jackson Square.*

In the 1840s, hundreds of Louisianians went off to Mexico to the Mexican War. One of these men brought the McIlhenny family of Avery Island some special Mexican pepper seeds. The result was Tabasco sauce, which now sells more than seventy million bottles annually, and can be found all over the world.

Avery Island is underlaid by a great salt dome that in places is within twelve feet of the surface. The rock salt mine is thought to be the first deposit discovered in the Western Hemisphere. This resource became crucial to preserve food for Confederate troops.

The Jungle Gardens and Bird City Sanctuary are two of the island's most remarkable features. The bird sanctuary was established in 1892 to protect the nearly extinct snowy egret. Now there are more than twenty-three thousand egrets and herons at nesting time, which peacefully coexist with alligator and deer. The gardens are resplendent with thousands of camellias, azaleas, and irises blooming in season from mid-fall to early summer.

From the Spanish period onward, no matter how poor, each south Louisiana household could easily grow one or two varieties of hot peppers. They realized that the flavor of foods, from old raccoon meat to "mud bugs," crawfish, were greatly enhanced by the addition of a little salt and a liberal dose of hot, red pepper.

Baton Rouge has been the state capital since 1880. It is the second-largest city in the state, and one of the nation's largest ports. Located at the northern end of the "Petrochemical Gold Coast," the industrial corridor that runs along the Mississippi upriver from New Orleans, the city is a neutral spot between north and south Louisiana. This is particularly appropriate since the name Baton Rouge means "red stick" or "red staff," referring to the tall cypress trees stripped of bark and coated with the blood of freshly killed animals, marking the boundary between the hunting grounds of two rival Indian tribes.

North Louisiana is yet another world from the southern part. It is dominated by the Red River, which bisects the state from northwest to southeast. Shreveport is the largest city in this part of the state and serves as its cultural center. The area in the nineteenth century didn't really amount to much until Henry Miller Shreve, a Yankee riverman, built the first steam snag boat and chugged up the Red River to clear out the 165-mile logjam that had blocked it for centuries. The entire Red River Valley is a monument to Shreve's achievement. Subsequently the United States government began to secure the fertile lands in the valley from the Caddo Indians. For a mere eighty thousand dollars the Indians gave up their lands, and then were promptly exiled from the United States.

Settlers began to pour in, snapping up rich cotton lands. Unlike the Creoles in the south, these new Louisianians were Anglo-Saxons from the eastern seaboard. They were hard-working Protestants, deeply rooted to the ideals of southern plantation society. Shreveport was the last major Confederate command to surrender in the Civil War. With this act on June 6, 1865, the conflict was officially ended.

Two of the other important cities of the area are Alexandria and Pineville, which sit across the Red River from each other. Alexandria was burned to the ground in 1864 by Union troops. Today the St. Francis Xavier Cathedral sits on the spot where Union General George Armstrong Custer's troops mutinied in 1865. During World War II seven million troops were trained near here under generals Eisenhower, Clark, and Patton. The Hotel Bentley was the site of many crucial summits to plan overseas strategies.

The northern part of Louisiana was not without its own proponents. The settling of the Red River Valley has been immortalized in many songs, one of which was "Oh, Susannah – I come from Alabama with a banjo on my knee. I'm going to Louisiana, my true love for to see." Another is *The Red River Valley*. Harriet Beecher Stowe also set her famed "Uncle Tom's Cabin" in the Red River Valley near Natchitoches.

Two things happened which brought the economic and political interests of north and south Louisiana closer together. The first was oil, and the second was Huey P. Long. In 1870 a night watchman at an ice plant in Shreveport accidently discovered natural gas when he struck a match over a newly distilled water well.

The monument to Senator Huey P. Long over his grave in the gardens of the State Capitol in Baton Rouge, which he had built.

Boats moored in one of Louisiana's many waterways.

Gas was soon used to provide illumination for the plant. By 1901 the first oil well was actively producing, and by 1908 the first pipeline was laid in the state. The offshore oil industry made many in south Louisiana instant millionaires. And oil money speaks loudly.

The exuberant spirit of Louisiana could not have been rekindled, however, had it not been for the revival that was started out in the wasted turnip fields of the northern red hill country of Winn Parish. While few Louisianians remember that theirs was the home state of President Zachary Taylor, they all remember that their native son "the Kingfish," Huey Long, almost challenged Franklin Delano Roosevelt for the American presidency.

Long was a backcountry, cottonseed-oil salesman who became a lawyer at the firm of Peters, Long and Strong in Baton Rouge. With the cunning of a rattlesnake, he changed the course of Louisiana forever. In his short eight years of power, he went as far as anyone before or since to make "every man a king" in Louisiana. The fact that most people during the Depression were willing "to swap a peck of freedom for a pint of a scarcity" got him elected governor, and then elected to the Senate in Washington. The rest of the South watched jealously as Long built hospitals, roads, and bridges in Louisiana. Of course, he built the bridge that spans the Mississippi at Baton Rouge just a few feet lower than it needs to be, to prevent ocean-going vessels from traveling upriver to Mississippi and Arkansas. But he saw to it that all of the children in Louisiana got free education, free textbooks, and free lunches, and that got other politicians thinking. Then on September 8, 1935, Huey Long was shot on the steps of the state capitol, and his reign of populism ended.

117

Above: *the 1926* Delta Queen, *one of Mississippi's last steam boats.*
Right: *octagonal Longwood Mansion, Natchez, stands incomplete,*
as it was when construction on it ceased in 1861.

Mississippi

Mississippi, although primarily a rural state, has long been a cultural center within the Deep South. Nobel-Prize-winning author, William Faulkner, brought the life of post-Reconstruction Mississippi to the world in his novels, while Hodding Carter achieved a Pulitzer Prize for his heroic civil rights stand at a small-town Delta newspaper. It is the home state of Leontyne Price, Eudora Welty, Tammy Wynette, Oprah Winfrey, Craig Claiborne, James Earl Jones, Charley Pride, and Morgan Freeman. But perhaps the most well-known personage ever to have emerged from Mississippi is "The King" – Elvis Presley, who was born in a modest, white-frame house in Tupelo in 1935.

The Delta is the cradle of the blues. With musical roots in Africa, "hollered" chants in the fields created a vehicle of expression for slaves. The Delta's remote rural plantations and small towns gave birth to a music of harsh realism created by a race gone from slavery to hopelessness. W. C. Handy published the first blues sheet music across the Mississippi border in Memphis in 1912. Later, within a generation, many other down-home artists from Mississippi achieved worldwide renown, notably Muddy Waters, Lead Belly, Howlin' Wolf, B. B. King, and Bo Diddly.

There is a clean, green bustle to the rich, soft loess bluffs of the land and the black soil of the Delta. Springtime finds the countryside and woods aglow with dogwood, peach blossoms, and azaleas. The Magnolia State contains of the most fertile river valleys in the world, formed by the powerful

Above: *1848 Biloxi Lighthouse, electrified in 1926.*

Mississippi River and two of the most productive rivers in North America – the Tombigbee and the Pearl.

It was in 1541 near what is now Clarkesdale in the state of Mississippi that Hernando de Soto first discovered the Mississippi River, named after the Chippewa term meaning "Father of the Waters" or "Large River." This vast leviathan is as twisting and long as its name.

The French, led by Pierre le Moyne, Sieur d'Iberville, established the first permanent settlement in the Mississippi Valley at Ocean Springs in 1699. It wasn't until France, favoring Louisiana, ceded Mississippi in 1763 that English-speaking immigrants

became interested in the territory. It became a popular resettling point for people from the Carolinas, Virginia, and Georgia, who were eager for larger tracts of virgin land.

After the American Revolution, the United States took possession of the territory north of the thirty-first parallel; the region south of the line remained part of Spanish West Florida. Mississippi didn't achieve its present borders until it became the twentieth state in 1817.

When sectionalism led to the Civil War, Mississippi was the second of the southern states to secede, and one of its native senators, Jefferson Davis, became the president of the Confederacy. Davis had spent his

Left: *a heavy evening sun hangs like a burning ball over the Mississippi River.*

Right and below: *the* Delta Queen, *which still plies the Mississippi from Natchez. She was built in 1926 and is one of only two passenger-carrying steam boats left on the river.*

boyhood at "Rosemont" near Woodville, and had married Varina Howell in Natchez. It was back to Mississippi that he came in defeat, settling with his family on the Gulf Coast.

While cotton is no longer king, it certainly ranks as a member of the royal family. It remains the principal crop, especially in the Delta. Mississippi ranks second in the United States in the total production of cotton, and first in the production of long-staple cotton. Today the farmers raise everything from soybeans to catfish.

The world's first human heart and lung transplants were performed at the University of Mississippi Medical Center at Jackson, a facility internationally recognized for its innovative work in organ transplantation and hypertension research. All of the space shuttle engines are tested at the NASA facility on the Mississippi Gulf Coast.

The southern staples of pecan pie and pralines wouldn't be the same without native pecans. Pecan trees were indigenous to Mississippi and Alabama. The settlers learned to use them from the Natchez, Chickasaw, and Choctaw Indians of the Muskogee group, who used them in every way – from a stuffing for birds to a sauce for meat. Settlers in Natchez became so attached to them that they used sugared pecans in their coffee as a sweetener.

Mississippi is a state filled with famous locations. The Natchez Trace, a trail over eight thousand years old, was worn through the wilderness by herds of mammals and Indian hunters, then trampled into a crude roadway by frontiersmen, trappers, soldiers of fortune, traders, evangelists, and "Kaintucks" – the men from the mountains to the northwest who floated iron, foodstuffs, tobacco, and manufactured goods down the Mississippi on flatboats. Once down river they sold their cargos, boats and all, and walked back home on the Trace. By 1806 the United States government sent men to widen the path into an actual road. It was by this route that Andrew Jackson and his Tennessee troops came to and from the famed Battle of New Orleans in 1812. By the 1820s the advent of the steamboat created an alternative route to the north. Port Gibson, located on Bayou Pierre, was one of

121

Spring Pilgrimage at Dunleith House, Natchez.

The costume room for the Confederate Pageant.

the prime stop-over points on the route. It was here that the first library in Mississippi was chartered in 1818. The Trace goes from Natchez, Mississippi, to Nashville, Tennessee. It is now maintained by the National Park Service, and is second only to the Blue Ridge Parkway as the most traveled parkway in the country.

Natchez is one of those cities whose very name exemplifies all the spirit and grandeur that the Old South stood for, yet in truth it is more like a small empire unto itself. It is the oldest and highest city on the Mississippi River. The Frenchman, Bienville, colonized the area in 1716, but it was the English and Spanish who brought the city its splendor late in the eighteenth century. It had its own silversmiths and the oldest cathedral in Mississippi. The infamous Natchez Under-the-Hill was the "Sodom on the Mississippi" from the 1700s. It was here that duels were fought, and where the Bowie knife was first used.

During the Revolutionary War Natchez was the fourteenth colony, though it was Tory in character. By 1832 the town lots in Natchez had a greater value than all of the rest of the land in the state. The Civil War saw Natchez with more millionaires per capita than any other city in America. During this time the Confederate flag never flew over Natchez, since many of its wealthy "nabobs" were English, Scottish, or Connecticut born. It was here that Ulysses S. Grant set up his headquarters for the Battle of Vicksburg.

During the Depression, the women of Natchez rallied behind Catherine Grafton Miller when she devised a plan to woo tourist dollars to save the antebellum treasures of Natchez. She donned a hoop skirt and toured the country on the bus, inviting people to visit the city "where the old South still lives." The success of the Natchez Pilgrimage has spawned a plethora of pilgrimages and spring garden tours throughout the state.

Today Natchez has one of the highest concentrations of restored antebellum buildings in the South. Pilgrimage has grown to a multi-million dollar industry, still controlled by the dedicated ladies of the Garden Club, who volunteer untold hours to treat guests to a taste of the "old" South.

The Spaniards settled Vicksburg on the bluff two hundred feet above the Mississippi in 1790. They named the town Nogales after the black walnut trees that grew there. During the Civil War, the city became known as the "Gibraltar of the South." The siege of Vicksburg ended when the city fell on July 4, 1863. Consequently, no proud southerner feels that there is too much to celebrate on that "black" day. In 1894 a Vicksburg candy merchant changed the course of soft drink history when he became the first person to bottle Coca-Cola.

The capital of Mississippi since 1821 has been centrally located Jackson, the state's largest city. Situated at the site of a trading post at Le Fleur's Bluff on the Pearl River and named for General Andrew Jackson, it is a remarkable monument to the New South. Mississippi has the second largest number of black elected officials in the country.

Mississippians are very cosmopolitan in their use of big cities. Those in the northern part of the state hop across the border into Tennessee to go to Memphis to shop, go to the doctor, and enjoy a little culture. Southwestern Mississippians gravitate toward Louisiana and New Orleans, while southeastern Mississippians feel more at home in Mobile, Alabama. The proximity of the plantations to the Mississippi River and railroads gave the cotton gentry easy access to these cities and the culture and foods of England, France, and Italy.

The history of Waverly Plantation Mansion, a national historic landmark, serves as a microcosm of the changing fortunes of plantation society in Mississippi and throughout the Deep South. In 1830 Colonel George Hampton Young, a Columbia-educated

Below: *the military cemeteries of Vicksburg are furrowed with graves. Nearly 17,000 Union soldiers alone are buried in Vicksburg.*

lawyer and former member of the Georgia legislature, moved into a two-story log house on the Tombigbee River near West Point. He had come to the northern part of the state as the secretary to the United States land commissioner, and bought up land at $1.50 an acre. By 1852 he had created a fifty thousand-acre self-sustaining empire, one of the largest in America. He and his family built a stately, octagonal antebellum mansion, resplendent with the finest English and French furniture. There was an elegant covered swimming pool made of brick and marble. Chandeliers were illuminated by gas manufactured at Waverly by burning pine knots in a retort. Water was supplied to the kitchen by pipes from the artesian wells.

After the Civil War, life at Waverly went on at a slower pace. In 1893 the National Fox Hunt Association was created in the library. Then in 1913 the last of Colonel Young's sons died; the other children had long ago abandoned the home for more "modern" dwellings in urban centers.

The house sat rotting in a swamp of briars until 1961 when a young couple from the northern part of Mississippi discovered it. The restoration of the magnificent property has been their life's work ever since. In order to pay for the maintenance, they open their home to the public 365 days a year. Today the couple live at Waverly with no air conditioning and very little heat, but "they could not bear to see such a wonderful dream discarded."

Topographically Mississippi has fertile rolling hills and thick forests. There are 17.2 million acres of forests, ranking Mississippi as one of the top sources of hardwood timber in the nation. It is a forerunner in

Left: the Confederate Memorial, but one symbol of Mississippi's war-torn past.

Below: the delicate bloom of a magnolia flower.

Above: *Jackson, named for Major General Andrew Jackson, hero of the War of 1812 and the Battle of New Orleans.*

paper products and printing. Each month approximately eleven million copies of the *National Geographic* roll off the presses in Corinth. Near Flora there is a forest with 36-million-year-old petrified logs. Since 1926 Mississippi has also ranked as one of the top gas and oil producing states.

North Mississippi is hilly forest land, which yields an abundant supply of lumber, clay for bricks, and streams for fresh water and transportation. Woodall Mountain is the highest point in Mississippi, standing 806 feet above sea level. It became a popular site for settlers from New England and Virginia, who had exhausted their farmlands.

In 1821 Columbus, one of the principal towns in the area, established the state's first free public school

Above: *Jackson's Beaux-Arts State Capitol, built in 1903 and called the New Capitol.*

Right: *a dirt road leading off into the distance gives an idea of the expanse of this state.*

Above: *Beauvoir, Biloxi, once home to Jefferson Davis.*

Above: *a sign advertising a "painless dentist" – one of the many charms of Natchez.*

Left: *earthenware on display at the Walter Anderson Cottage, Ocean Springs.*

Facing page: *Tullis-Toledano Manor, Biloxi, built in 1856 by Christoval Toledano.*

system. Twenty years later, the first state-supported educational institution for women in the United States was founded, later becoming the Mississippi University for Women. Among southern women, the women of Columbus set a unique precedent. On April 25, 1866, a group of prominent ladies had a tea to commemorate Confederate "Decoration Day" to honor their war dead. While standing at the graveyard with their arms filled with flowers, one of the participants, a war widow, chose to place her flowers on the Union enemy graves. "After all," she stated, "these are some mothers' sons!"

Mississippi

Right off the shore, a part of the continental shelf, is a narrow string of islands with tranquil lagoons, swaying grasses, and land crisscrossed by winding streams. On Ship Island the brothers Bienville and Iberville landed in 1699. They chose the area between what is now Ocean Springs and Biloxi as the first capital of an area that stretched to Pennsylvania. At this settlement the French pioneers were given their first taste of the New World.

Down the beach is Pascagoula, which was given to the Duchess of Chaumont by Louis XIV. During prohibition it was noted as the home base of unsinkable rum-running vessels. In the 1930s the Ingalls Corporation arrived to create the largest shipbuilding yard in the South. It gained fame by producing the first all-welded seagoing ships.

"The Coast" is an eighty-mile strip of magic beachfront land on the Mississippi Gulf Coast that holds special summer memories for generations of children. Lines of moss-draped oaks, gardens of fragrant bougainvillaea and the bittersweet smell of oleander, and stately antebellum cottages with generous verandas overlook the scenic silver blue of the Gulf of Mexico. The original settlers were French, Spanish, and Mediterranean, those for whom the relaxed, maritime climate, the sun and gulf breezes were crucial. Coastal inhabitants are a bit "spicier," warmer, and more vibrant than those of Anglo-Saxon descent in the rest of the state. It is a world of ceremonies, parades, and lingering afternoon naps.

Below: *Biloxi's Gulf Coast, which has made the town a popular resort.*

Right: *Pass Christian, once a favorite vacation spot of Andrew Jackson.*

Above: *a crane silhouetted against the Gulf Coast of Alabama.*
Right: *a russet farm building in northeast Alabama.*

Alabama

Alabama epitomizes the successful southerner of the twenty-first century, a tycoon with blueblood sensibilities and plantation roots, complicated, sophisticated, brilliant, and high-spirited. On one hand, the state is eccentric with town names like Bug Tussle Gap on Highway 78 near Anniston; on the other, it is a state alive with innovation. Tuscumbia was the birthplace of Helen Keller, who single-handedly revolutionized the perception and care of the handicapped of the world. She was born at her grandfather's Ivy Green Cottage in 1880. In 1910 near Montgomery, the Wright brothers changed the way the world traveled when they opened the first school of aviation in the United States. Hank Williams, the creator of modern country music, was born in a log cabin in 1923. Today at Huntsville, the site of the first English settlement in the state, is NASA's Marshall Space Flight Center, the largest space museum in the world. Since 1965 the small town of Muscle Shoals has been one of the music industry's prime recording spots. Hundreds of entertainers as diverse as Peggy Lee and the Rolling Stones come here to energize their music with the Muscle Shoals sound.

Alabama has romantic roots. A widely circulated myth has it that a roving Welsh prince-explorer moved to Mobile Bay in the twelfth century and taught many of the Indians to speak Welsh. Whether or not it is true, Alabama does have a town named Lanfairpwllgwy.

Until it can be proved otherwise, however, the Spanish get the credit for discovering Alabama. Hernando de Soto and his band of five hundred Spaniards stumbled into the area in 1540 on their tenacious quest for gold. They had heard reports from Spanish adventurers who had visited the Alabama coast as early as 1505. They claimed "the people wear hats of solid gold and life is gay and luxurious."

The Indians they encountered were of a highly-evolved culture over ten thousand years old. In western Alabama there is a large concentration of mounds at Moundville, which stretches out along the state's river systems. Archeological research reveals remnants of a trade economy with copper from the north and shells from the Gulf. The name Alibamu, which in Choctaw describes the brushgatherer tribe, is still used today in reference to the state. After the Spaniards massacred Chief Tuscaloosa and thousands of Indians on October 18, 1540, little else remained of the rich Indian culture.

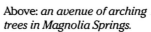

Above: *an avenue of arching trees in Magnolia Springs.*

Right: *the State Capitol, Montgomery, where Jefferson Davis was inaugurated.*

It wasn't until the French trappers created Fort Louis in 1702 near Mobile that a permanent colony was established. The new settlers began cultivating the coastal land for rice and indigo. By 1719 these farmers had prospered to the extent that they began to bring slave labor to help them. There continued to be French infusions of population in Alabama until the mid-nineteenth century. Defeated followers of Napoleon founded the settlement of Demopolis in 1817. They reasoned, after much study of climate and soil, that this would be an ideal place to create vineyards and grow Mediterranean olives. Their crops failed, however, and their Celtic neighbors were hostile; so the Bonapartist settlers moved on to other enterprises in other Alabama towns.

Alabama became the twenty-second state in the Union in 1819, though Montgomery wasn't chosen to be the capital until 1847. It is located near the center

of the state, near natural shipping lanes and in the center of the fertile cotton-growing plain.

Most Alabamians are fierce states'-righters. The state motto remains, *Audemus Jura Nostra Defendere*, "We Dare to Defend our Rights." The very announcement of abolitionist Abraham Lincoln's ascendancy to the presidency led the state to be instrumental in the creation of a new nation, the Confederate States of America. The Ordinance of Secession was passed in Montgomery in 1861, and Jefferson Davis was elected as president. "The man and the hour have met" was the way in which he was introduced at his inauguration in February 1861. Two weeks later the granddaughter of former President Tyler raised the newly created Confederate flag over the capitol. The telegram that changed the course of southern life forever was sent from here in April 1861, when Davis issued the order to fire on Fort Sumter.

Montgomery was the capital of the Confederate States of America for a short time, until it was moved to Richmond, Virginia, in May 1861.

The women of Montgomery still pride themselves on their many autochthonous high-brow societies. Clubs such as Hypatia, New Era, and Tintagil date back to Reconstruction days. Of course, they aren't nearly so snobbish as the thirteen Montgomery gentlemen who even refuse to speak the name of their learned group to those outside the families of their membership.

After 1915 the destruction of the cotton economy caused a migration of blacks to the cities in hopes of finding jobs in the new industries. These new urban blacks had a powerful voice. It was here that the first victory in the Civil Rights struggle was achieved in 1955 with the Montgomery Bus Boycott. Dr. Martin Luther King, Jr., a newly ordained local preacher, was

one of its organizers. It is interesting that today January 1 is the day set aside in the state to celebrate both Martin Luther King's and Robert E. Lee's birthdays.

As in many other southern states, cotton was the prime economic force; but unlike other states, Alabama yielded iron and coal in the Birmingham area. Furthermore, colossal hydroelectric projects of the Tennessee Valley Authority helped pull northern Alabama out of the throes of the post-Reconstruction depression.

Birmingham is Alabama's largest city. The crossing for the South and North Railroad and the Alabama and Chattanooga Railroads in 1870 in the center of Jones Valley, it brought the sleepy 1813 settlement of "Red Sticks" to life. Shrewd speculators had just to look at the red hills to see the iron hematite. It seemed that the combination of the railroads, coal, iron, limestone, and a large work force created the booming metropolis of Birmingham overnight. More than fifty blast furnaces were producing steel by 1890. It wasn't until the boom waned during the 1929 Depression that the settler-industrialists set about to catch their breaths and lay out gracious tree-lined residential areas.

Facing page: *Hull Street Historic District, Montgomery.*

Below: *rocking chairs on a front porch in Opelika.*

Above: *Liberty holds her flame aloft over Birmingham.*

Left: *Birmingham grew tall by producing iron. Now her major employer is the University.*

Right: *ducks flying over the Decatur National Wildlife Reserve.*

Below: *grass-tufted sand dunes in Gulf State Park.*

The city is dominated by the statue of Vulcan, which sits atop a 124-foot pedestal on Red Mountain. The mythical god of metallurgy was made out of native Alabama iron for the 1904 Louisiana Purchase Exhibition in St. Louis. The statue is said to have originally held a bulging jar of dill pickles in his hand; today, however, he holds a lamp that burns green as long as Birmingham drivers obey the rules of the road and red if there is a fatality.

The landscape of Alabama varies drastically from the Appalachian hill country of the northeast to the bayou lands near Mobile and the sandy beaches, as white and fine as sugar, near Gulf Shores. The majority of the land of the state is made up of a loamy coastal plain. Sylacauga, in the southwest corner of the Talladega National Forest, is famous for its marble quarry from which the marble came that was used to build the United States Supreme Court Building.

The population is just as varied. There are the pinewood Creoles with a mixture of Indian, Spanish, French, and English blood; the Old South gentry of Mobile, Selma, Montgomery, and Tuscaloosa; and the cosmopolitan residents of Huntsville and Birmingham.

In the northern part of Alabama, Cheaha Mountain rises 2,407 feet above sea level. Settlers arrived in this area at the fringe of the Appalachian Mountains from the Carolinas, Tennessee, and Kentucky. These Celtic descendants were independent rural farmers, who, when faced with secession, chose instead to set up their own pro-Union state of Nickajack. This group was so anti-Confederate that the ruthless William T. Sherman chose these Nickajackians for his personal bodyguards.

139

Above: *the unusual Boll Weevil Statue, Enterprise.*　　　Right: *the President's Mansion, Tuscaloosa.*

Through the center of Alabama runs the fertile 4,300-square-mile limestone and marl soil region known as the Black Belt. The cotton gin came here as early as 1800, transforming what were broad, tree-lined plains into some of the richest cotton fields in the world. By the time of the Civil War, roughly eighty percent of the population of the area were slaves. After the war many stayed on as tenant farmers until the boll weevil came in 1915, forcing crop diversification.

Enterprise, Alabama, can boast the only monument in the world to the boll weevil, the tiny Mexican snout-nosed beetle that destroyed the South's economy when it wiped out the cotton crop in 1915. As a result, the farmers in this county experimented with other crops and discovered that peanuts would rebuild their fortunes. The monument was constructed in 1919 "in profound appreciation to the boll weevil and what it has done to herald prosperity."

At the emotional heart of the Black Belt is the town of Tuscaloosa, home of the University of Alabama. The

town took its name from the Choctaw word for "black warrior." Tuscaloosa, founded in 1816, was originally the capital of the state. The wealthy, plantation-based economy allowed the citizens the resources to aggrandize their city by planting water oaks along the streets, thus causing the city to be called "Druid City."

The soul of the Black Belt can be said to be the town of Selma, perched high atop the bluffs of the Alabama River. It was named for a place in a Gaelic poem. Sophisticated and flamboyant plantation society flourished here with magnificent houses and a thoroughbred racing season famous throughout the South. In 1965 the eyes of the world watched the confrontation between African-Americans and the remnants of privileged plantation society as it played out on the Edmond Pettus Bridge.

One Alabama landmark of the post-slavery period is the famed Tuskegee Institute, founded in 1881 by the acclaimed African-American scholar, Booker T. Washington. The campus was constructed by the black students, former slaves, and sons of slaves from bricks they had made themselves. It was here in 1896 that the renowned black scientist, Dr. George

Left: *De Soto State Park.*

Below: *one of Alabama's lovely churches.*

Alabama

Above: *a prairie near Uniontown blooming in spring.*

Above left: *deer roaming the forests of northeast Alabama.*

Left: *red-tufted winter fields near Tuskegee.*

Washington Carver, head of the agriculture department, made his discoveries involving the many uses of the peanut.

Mobile (pronounced MO-beel) is a city like no other. It was named for the Maubilla Indians who were already living in the area. Jean-Baptiste le Moyne, Sieur de Bienville, created the first permanent white settlement in Alabama here in 1702. Bienville celebrated the first Mardi Gras in the United States in1703. For many years Mobile was the capital of France's vast Louisiana Territory. From its port, second only in size to New Orleans, timber and cotton were shipped all over the world. By the Civil War sixty-five percent of all foreigners in Alabama lived in Mobile. They imparted a sense of old-world sensibility.

The French also brought in the oriental, ornamental flower called the azalea. Today there are millions of varieties of azaleas ranging in color from white to fuchsia. Those planted in the nineteenth century are over twenty feet tall. The streets are lined with majestic double files of oaks, iron-galleried buildings designed by Spaniards and Frenchmen, and magnificent, white-columned Greek Revival homes dating from the glory days of the antebellum South.

The spirit of Mobile is unflappable. After Reconstruction had begun in 1866, when things looked their bleakest, Joseph Cain, a clerk in a Mobile market, decided it was time to resurrect the spirit of Mardi Gras. He and a band of cronies gathered and rolled themselves in soot, red clay, and Spanish moss. "Chief Slackabamirmico and His Lost Cause Minstrels" drove

Above: *a stilted platform in Mobile Bay.*

Left: *a Mobile port worker loading soyabeans for export.*

Right: *delicate camellia blooms.*

through the streets of Mobile in a decorated charcoal wagon, clanging cowbells. The mayor had them in for a drink, and the Mobile Mardi Gras was reborn.

The city's economy got a boost when one of the largest natural gas deposits in the United States was discovered under Mobile Bay. The Alabama State Docks were the first completely state-owned facility for the handling of freight. The Alabama Dry Dock and Shipbuilders Corporation is the largest on the Gulf Coast.

Walter Bellingrath's estate created in 1918 in Theodore, twenty miles from Mobile, is a luxurious example of Mobile's love of flowers. Bellingrath, a new Coca-Cola millionaire, was the son of a German immigrant father and a Scotch-Irish mother. He and his wife, "Miss Bessie," were captivated by the gardens they saw in Europe. They came home with ideas to create the grandest garden in Alabama. This eight hundred-acre estate is the epitome of a lush subtropical paradise with giant live oaks draped with

Spanish moss, an exotica conservatory, a camellia parterre exhibiting over five thousand varieties, and acres of hydrangeas, crepe myrtle, and wisteria. The Bellingraths left the garden to a foundation which provides funds to many colleges and churches throughout the South.

When the state of Alabama was formed, the Gulf Shore became the thin stretch cut from the Florida panhandle to allow access to the sea. The culinary benefits from this piece of land are remarkable, including pampano, a flat, silver-blue fish with a sweet sea flavor, and fat red snappers. Mobile is known for its delicious invention, the West Indies Salad, an iced, marinated crabmeat dish.

The Alabama version of southern cuisine has long been considered one of the best in the South. The moist, fruit-nut-filled Lane Cake was the choicest culinary treat of the United States at the turn of the century. It was invented by Emma Rylander Lane of Clayton, Alabama, who published the trend-setting *Good Things To Eat* in 1898.

Above: *a charming Arkansas farm in a yellow-tipped field.*
Right: *the capital Little Rock on the Arkansas River.*

Arkansas

There is a great deal more to Arkansas than its fearsome razorbacks or the fact that it is where "Li'l Abner's" hometown of Dogpatch USA is located. Arkansas towns have names unique to this state – Old Joe, Tomato, Delight (pronounced DE-lite), Ben Hur, Bald Knob, Toad Suck, Tabletop, Strawberry, and Foggy Bottom, to name but a few. America's largest cotton plantation and some of the country's wealthiest men call Arkansas home. It is the home state of noted philanthropist, William Fulbright. Nelson Rockefeller's brother, Winthrop, was a former governor of the state and a leading rancher and industrialist. His home, Petit Jean (pronounced Petty Gene), was located on an impressive, cattle-breeding farm. The magnificent barns house both cattle and an extensive collection of antique automobiles. The barns are so elegant that one visitor wrote in the guestbook, "Oh, to be a cow!"

Small agricultural communities such as Arkadelphia, Searcy, Camden, Jonesboro, Pine Bluff, and Newport possess an aristocratic, yet hard-working Protestant farmer gentry. Along with the work ethic comes a quiet appreciation for quality education and civic pride.

Arkansas has long been noted for its spas. Since the early nineteenth century, the sterile, thermal waters of Hot Springs have been sought by people from all over the world. By 1832 the federal government had set aside the springs and surrounding area as the country's first unofficial national park. The famed natural springs flow from the outcrop of sandstone on the west slope of Hot Springs Mountain. Within a twelve-acre radius are close to fifty springs with a flow that varies from 750,000 to 950,000 gallons a day. Beginning as rainwater that is absorbed

Above: *Bathhouse Row in Hot Springs National Park.*

Above: steam rising in Hot Springs National Park.

into the mountains northeast of the park, the water then flows down to eight thousand feet underground, where the heat of the earth raises its temperature to 143 degrees Fahrenheit. This process is thought to take about four thousand years.

The altitude of Hot Springs National Park varies from six hundred feet on the valley floor to fourteen hundred feet along the summit. It is unusual as national parks go because it is surrounded by the thriving city of Hot Springs.

In the city of Hot Springs elaborate Italianate bathhouses lined the main streets of the town. Next to

New Orleans, Hot Springs had the most famous red-light district in the South. It was frequented by horse-racing afficionados. For most of the twentieth century Hot Springs was the only place in Arkansas where liquor could be legally served. During its heyday, health seekers and those seeking a yearly "drying out" took the waters by day, and could enjoy gambling and concerts in the evenings. Going to the lavish spa, however, was not without its hazards. Wealthy turn-of-the-century tourists were terrorized by the criminal talents of the likes of Jesse James, the Dalton Gang, and Belle Starr. Some of their most famous heists took place in the vicinity of Hot Springs.

Eureka Springs was an ancient Indian spa visited for its special health-giving properties. On July 4, 1879, Dr. Alvah Jackson and several hundred followers established a healing center here. By 1883 the railroad brought visitors from all over the east coast. Prohibitionist Carrie Nation lived in this community and made her final temperance speech here.

The advent of modern medicine caused a rapid decline in the use of the spa. Today visitors come for recreation, to view an extensive artists' colony of Ozark craftsmen, and for spiritual growth. The town could almost be mistaken for Las Vegas from a distance, yet up close each motel along the main strip has a Bible verse on its marquee. The Great Passion Play depicts Christ's last week on earth through the resurrection and ascension. The elaborate staging area replicates the streets and region around Jerusalem. Another landmark is the Christ of the Ozarks, a remarkable seven-story statue that weighs over one million pounds. The sculpture towers over Magnetic Mountain with its outstretched arms measuring sixty-five feet from hand to hand.

Mammoth Spring is thought to be one of the nation's largest springs, its flow counted at nine million gallons of water per hour. Legend has it that the spring was discovered by an Indian chief who dug a grave for his son who had died during a drought.

Left: a display of craftwork at the Ozark Folk Center, part of the state parks system.

Facing page: the graceful interior of Fordyce Bathhouse on Central Avenue in Hot Springs National Park.

When the east coast of America was involved in the Revolutionary War, Arkansas was still a wilderness where few white men had ventured. The state lies west of the Mississippi River, with one foot in the Old West and the other in the Deep South. The renowned spas, remote mountains, and rich delta country add texture to the 53,104-square-mile state.

Rich in natural resources, Arkansas is home to the only diamond mine in the United States, located in Murfreesboro in Pike County. The first diamond was unearthed in 1906, and since then over seventy

Left: *a house in the historic Quapaw Quarter of Little Rock, famous for its homes.*

Right: *beautiful, sun drenched Boxley Valley in the Ozark National Forest.*

Below: *two canoeists on the Buffalo River.*

thousand diamonds and other semi-precious stones have been found. The park is open to the public, and a recent visitor found a seventeen-carat diamond, which he was allowed to keep.

The north central part of the state is known for limestone and marble, as well as coal and manganese mines. Oil and natural gas are found in the south in the Arkansas River Valley. Arkansas is also known for bauxite, the source of aluminum. Ninety percent of America's supply comes from an area near Little Rock. One Miss Arkansas contestant in the Miss America Pageant in the 1960s wore a dress in the evening gown competition made entirely of aluminum foil. The Hot Springs region is rich in quartz crystals of superb brilliance. Locally mined novaculite is used all over the world as industrial whetstone.

The state is an agricultural paradise. Rice thrives in the swampy, southeast lowlands between the Arkansas and Mississippi rivers. In the northwest of the state are lush wheat fields and apple orchards. Arkansas is known for award-winning watermelons, some of which weigh as much as two hundred

A logger working on the Buffalo River.

pounds. The state has six native varieties of trees. Yellow pine accounts for sixty percent of the state's lumber income. Arkansas also leads the nation in the production of red gum, oak, and hickory.

Berryville is called "The Turkey Capital of Arkansas," with over half a million gobblers bred there yearly. There is an eight-foot-tall, blue concrete and stucco statue of a turkey in the center of town. The Catfish Farmers of America are headquartered in

Little Rock. Arkansas catfish are shipped to markets from Japan to Sweden. One of the world's largest bottlers of mountain spring water is in Hot Springs.

It is thought that Hernando de Soto was the first white visitor to Arkansas. On May 12, 1541, he and his exhausted band of explorers pulled up on the east bank of the Mississippi River near the area of Sunflower Landing below the present town of Helena. Marquette and Joliet were actually the first to see the potential of the lands west of the Mississippi River on their visit to Arkansas over a century later in 1673. The Jesuit priest, Jacques Marquette, had been assigned by the king to accompany the fur trader, Louis Joliet, to find where the river emptied into the sea. These two Frenchmen and five Indians had come canoeing down the river from Lake Michigan. They turned back at the mouth of the Arkansas River, having heard rumors of hostile Indians down river. The land was formally claimed by France on April 9, 1682, by Robert Cavalier, Sieur de la Salle. Arkansas' first European settlement followed in 1686 with the establishment of a fort at the mouth of the Arkansas

Below: *a wooden building in the Buffalo National River area, surrounded by trees.*

Facing page: *a wall display in Brack's General Store, Kingston.*

Above: *a fisherman on Lake Ouachita as the sun sinks.*

Below: *fall colors darn the Ouachita Mountains.*

River. Arkansas Post continued to be a thriving port between the other French settlements in Louisiana and those in Canada until the late eighteenth century.

John Law, in 1717, sold the French Government a development scheme that came to be known as the "Mississippi Bubble." The Scotsman proposed a settlement of six thousand white Europeans served by half as many African slaves. Law staked claim to twenty-five hundred square miles around Arkansas Post and advertised the friendliness of the Indians: "The beauty of the climate has a great influence on the character of the inhabitants, who are at the same time very gentle and very brave. They have ever had an enviable friendship with the French uninfluenced thereto either by fear or views of interest; and live with them as brethren rather than neighbors."

In 1763 France ceded Arkansas to Spain. Then the French got it back, and sold it to the United States as part of the Louisiana Purchase in 1803. In the spring of 1804, Lt. James B. Many of the United States Army ran up the Stars and Stripes at Arkansas Post. By act of the legislature of Tennessee on June 27, 1806, the lower part of the District of New Madrid, two-thirds of the present state of Arkansas, was designated the District of "Arkansaw."

Soon veterans of the War of 1812 were eagerly flocking to the new frontier. By July 4, 1819, the territory had achieved territorial status with fourteen thousand settlers. Arkansas had first been attached to the Louisiana Territory, and then to the Missouri Territory. It didn't gain sufficient population to become a territory on its own until 1819.

The Missouri Compromise of 1820 was based on the deal by which Missouri could be admitted to the Union as a slave state and Maine as a free state. Also, the line between free and slave territories was set at the line thirty-six degrees thirty minutes at Arkansas' northern border. The capital was moved to Little Rock in 1821. On June 15, 1836, Arkansas became the twelfth state to be admitted to the Union subsequent to the formation of the original thirteen colonies.

Early settlers discovered a modern-day Eden. The Arkansas River, fresh and free-flowing, had many streams which cut an easy passage for families and their belongings through the rugged terrain of the state. It was a land of abundant rainfall and mild winters, vast grazing herds, and migratory birds. Buffalo, elk, and deer roamed the valleys, while black bear inhabited the ridges. Spectacular lakes and streams are today filled with black bass and catfish. Stuttgart, at the heart of the rice-producing Grand Prairie, is still considered one of the greatest duck hunting and fishing areas in North America. Each year the International Duck-Calling Championships are held here.

The Ozark Plateau is at the elevated northwestern

Sunrise over Arkansas' Ouachita Mountains.

portion of the state. It is separated by the Arkansas River and its fertile valley floor from the Ouachita Mountains. The highest points in the state are found in these mountains, where Mt. Magazine and several other major summits exceed twenty-seven hundred feet above sea level. It is the highest peak between the Rockies and the Alleghenies. The Ouachita Mountains are unique in that they run east-west rather than in the north-south direction of most American ranges. Today the Ouachita National Forest lies in west central Arkansas, and spreads into southeastern Oklahoma. The Ozark National Forest totals over a million acres in the Boston and Ozark mountains in northwestern Arkansas. Cove Lake, a 160-acre mountain lake southeast of the town of Paris, is the highest point in Arkansas. Booneville in south Logan

County is unique in that it shares a county seat with Paris, one of the state's few "wet" cities. The area produces a large number of America's bowling balls.

The wilderness land of the "District of Arkansaw" attracted diverse groups of people, each seeking their own private ideals. Clannish Scotch-Irish from the southern Appalachians gravitated to the areas most like those they had left. Before coming to the New World, these people had been twice dispossessed in Scotland and Ireland. They were hard-working, tenacious, proud, and determined to survive. They were devoutly Protestant, and it is said that they kept the Sabbath – and everything else they could get their hands on.

They settled in, nestled in a labyrinth of Ozark and Ouchita vales. These were a people isolated culturally and geographically, who were inward and self-sufficient. Their traditions ran deep. This can still be

Facing page: *mail boxes in Buffalo National River district.*

Above: *a painted barn in the Ozark Mountains.*

seen and heard today in the remote areas where the music, art, food, and legends bespeak life in their sixteenth- and seventeenth-century homelands.

The wild west frontier attracted proponents of howling frontier values. One independent frontiersman was Sam Houston, the future president of the Lone Star Republic of Texas. Houston, a former governor of Tennessee, left his family and position in the 1830s to carouse with his Cherokee Indian pals and run a trading post in the Arkansas woods.

Van Buren and Fort Smith became the major outfitting points for prospectors seeking gold and for soldiers on the way to fight Indians or going to the Mexican War. Fort Smith was the home of Judge Isaac Parker, the notorious "hanging judge" and "Yellow Dog Democrat," so called because of his Republican tendencies.

The fertile Mississippi bottomlands of the southeast attracted fortune-seeking farmers who wanted cotton to transform them into millionaires. Many farmer-soldiers came to the territory seeking large tracts of cheap land like the spreads they had heard of in Virginia, Georgia, and South Carolina. Within one generation, these newly aristocratic planters had the wealth and power to enable them to influence the majority of the electorate of the state into following their interests.

Plantations were created in locations which afforded the planters easy access to the Mississippi River. This provided economic and cultural links to the Gulf of Mexico and continental parts beyond.

These various factions of settlers made Arkansas' statehood a hotly contested issue between up-country and low country. Slaveholding was, for the most part, done on a smaller scale in Arkansas than in other southern states. Almost half of the slaves in the territory worked for farmers who owned fewer than five slaves. The issue that split the state was a matter of taxation. The Scotch-Irish were not pleased with parting with a cent of their income. Their land on the Ozark plateau was too poor to sustain more than dirt farms, due to the short growing season. Corn was grown to be used in "moonshine," white lightning, the staple crop of "dry" counties.

Slavery and Confederate values did not become an issue until President Lincoln demanded troops to fight the South. On May 20, 1861, Arkansas decided to join the Confederacy. The voting population of Arkansas was only about sixty thousand in 1860, yet records show that fifty thousand men entered the Confederate service, while another thirteen thousand joined the Union forces.

Present-day Arkansas is a blend of tradition, fundamentalism, progressive economic politics, and a deep-seated love of nature. Little Rock is known as the "City of Roses," and is the largest city in the state. It was founded on a ridge overlooking the Arkansas River. From its very beginnings as the central point in the state, its populace exemplified a desire to live well.

By 1840, although Little Rock's population was only about fifteen hundred, the city was filled with grand buildings and its aristocracy imported citrus fruits and shellfish from the Gulf. By 1860 it was an active port city with the largest flour mill west of the Mississippi, three newspapers, an elegant hotel, a college, and a female seminary.

In the 1880s a street was named after the late President Lincoln. Victorian mansions of the nouveau riche Yankees soon lined the street. Even today, old Little Rock families refer to the street as "Robber's Row."

Each community honors its traditions in a variety of ways. Mountain View is the cultural crossroads of the Ozarks. The Old-Time Fiddlers Association State Championship Competition and the Southern Regional Mountain and Hammer Dulcimer Workshops and Contests are just two of the many festivals held in the small folk center.

The King Biscuit Blues Festival takes place each October in the small town of Helena. Although this is a small town, it has a diverse musical heritage. It was the hometown of blues singer Sonny Boy Williams, country singer Conway Twitty (Harold Jenkins), and lyric soprano Frances Greer.

Left: *a guide shows children around Pinnacle Mountain State Park near Little Rock.*

Facing page: *fiddles on display at the Ozark Folk Center – lovely examples of local crafts.*

Above: *dogwood flowers, a common sight in Arkansas.*

Above: *taking the sun at Fort Lauderdale, Florida.*
Right: *the magnificent white beach at Hollywood.*

Florida

Within the family of southern states, Florida is the renegade black sheep, the soldier of fortune. Great contrasts prevail. It is world famous for its palm-fringed, white sand beaches; the Daytona 500 auto race; Disneyworld; Sanibel Island, considered one of the world's best shelling beaches; and its citrus industry. Yet there is more to Florida. The soul of the antebellum South still inhabits the northern part of the state; the new industrial and agricultural South thrives in central and southern Florida; and there are still old-world Mediterranean enclaves throughout the state.

Cape Canaveral, near Orlando, is the heart of the American space program. The John F. Kennedy Space Center is where the first U.S. space satellite was launched in 1958. In 1961 Alan Shepard and Gus Grissom left from there to become the first and second Americans to fly in space. Apollo II lifted off in 1969 for the first manned landing on the moon.

In sharp contrast is the small Aegean fishing village of Tarpon Springs, just north of St. Petersburg. Here Greek fishermen with black eyes and black mustaches climb aboard their brightly painted broad boats bearing names from ancient Greece – the *Pericles*, the *Aphrodite* – to gather sponges, skeletons which are part plant, part animal.

Florida, the Sunshine State, is dedicated to a search for paradise. Its population is made up of thousands of people who have moved there seeking

Above: *Tarpon Springs – famous for its sponges*

Left: *the John and Mable Ringling Museum of Art in Sarasota.*

Above: *the Ringling Museum of Art, famous for its collection of Baroque works.*

sun and relaxation. As a matter of fact, only thirty-five percent of Floridians were actually born there.

One man who epitomized the state's spirit of exuberance was the world-renowned circus impresario, John Ringling. Like many other Floridians, Ringling was born a Yankee, one of the eight children of a German father and an Alsatian mother, raised in Baraboo, Wisconsin. At sixteen he joined several of his brothers to form a "Classic and Comic Concert Company." Ultimately the brothers were to buy up other small circuses until they had swallowed up all their rivals and amassed "The Greatest Show on Earth": The Ringling Brothers, Barnum & Bailey Circus. By 1920 Ringling was one of the richest men on earth. Old-timers in Sarasota remember Ringling as a quiet, dapper man with a cane and a crisp, unlit cigar. His wife, Mable, a native of Moons, Ohio, was a kind, unpretentious woman described by friends as being "cozy."

Mable and John Ringling did travel, and Mable developed a passion for Venice. It seemed quite a sensible idea to move all of the European elements she liked to Florida. The house they built is one of America's greatest monuments to fanciful opulence. In 1924 they commissioned architect James Baum to create a mansion which would resemble the Doge's Palace in Venice. Mable also liked the design of her husband's New York building, Madison Square Garden, so stylistic elements of it, too, were added. The house, called Ca'd'Zan, meant House of John in the Venetian dialect. It was so overwhelming that native Sarasotans remarked that it was enough to make the "Doges howl!"

The youthful spirit of Florida's culture may have something to do with its geological beginnings. Florida is a distinctive appendage, the most geographically southern state in the United States and the geological "baby" of the continent, because it was the last part of the land to rise from the ocean. Today Florida's highest point is only 345 feet above sea level and is located in the northern part of the state near Lakewood. The bed of limestone on which Florida rests reaches a depth of eighteen thousand feet in a few places. It includes a labyrinth of subterranean streams and caves, which explains the phenomenon of lakes which disappear overnight only to reappear a few days later. There are more than thirty thousand lakes ranging from mere puddles to the seven hundred-square-mile Lake Okeechobee. In addition, there are twenty-seven artesian springs and fifteen hundred rivers and creeks.

On the Atlantic side there are long, slender, white sand barrier beaches, which enclose the Intracoastal Waterway. At St. Lucie Inlet this busy marine highway divides, with one branch running south to Key West and the other crossing the peninsula through the St. Lucie Canal to Lake Okeechobee and the Caloosahatchee River to Fort Myers. The west coast is deeply indented with bays, which begin south of the Suwannee River. The low, marshy land fades into the Ten Thousand Islands along the sea edge of the Everglades.

Florida is a naturalist's paradise with fifteen varieties of palm native to the state. It is the only state in the Union with both indigenous alligators and crocodiles. There is the rare Torrey Yucca tree and

Flamingoes, once a very common sight in Florida.

Florida yew, which grow along the Apalachicola River west of Tallahassee. The state animal is the native panther. In the everglades region there are over four hundred varieties of birds, including the pink flamingo and the snowy egret.

Aboriginal people are thought to have first settled in the area about twelve thousand years ago. By 500 B.C. the tribes in the northern part of the state had begun to cultivate corn, while the southern tribes remained gatherers and hunters.

Those who think America began with the English settlers will be surprised to learn that St. Augustine is the oldest permanent European settlement in the United States. It was Spain's capital of its Florida empire and its principal stronghold north of Mexico. In one generation the Spanish had created the largest empire in the world, stretching from the Andes to mid-North America.

St. Augustine became the center for an enclave of Spaniards who had vast sugar, silver, gold, and shipping fortunes. There was a close relationship between the coastal cities and the West Indies, which can be seen in the architecture. By 1706 the Spaniards had brought their version of the Renaissance to North America. The classical columns of the governor's

Above: *musket drill at Castillo de San Marcos, the oldest structure in Saint Augustine.*

Right: *the Spanish/Moorish Flagler College on King Street, Saint Augustine.*

palace in St. Augustine made it a far grander structure than the staid dwellings in the English colonies of New England.

After 1734, verandas were added to the colonists' cottages,which in the 1830s were further embellished with the classical touches of the Greek Revival. Today the stuccoed walls of the old buildings of St. Augustine proudly wear the sun- and rain-blistered scars of centuries of existence. The lush bougainvillaea, palm, and hibiscus that line the streets provide an inescapable Latin texture.

For most of the sixteenth century the Spanish, French, and English competed over which country would gain superiority over what they thought was a large island. John Cabot, an Englishman, recorded his visit to Florida in 1498. The Spaniard, Juan Ponce de Leon, who had accompanied Columbus on his second voyage, came back to explore in 1513 in search of the fountain of youth and gold.

He and his party landed in the spring, finding an orgy of flowers and wildlife. As it was Easter (Pascua Florida in Spanish), he named the land Florida. Early battles with the native Indians convinced the Spaniards that they were near the gold they had come for. On Saint Augustine's Day, September 8, 1565, the first permanent Florida outpost was established in a town named for the saint. This was forty-two years before the ill-fated British colony in Jamestown, Virginia.

The fertile lands of northern Florida made it very much a part of the southern plantation economy of the eighteenth to mid-nineteenth century, while southern Florida remained isolated until the advent of the railroad in the late nineteenth century. Florida was

Above: *a passageway in Seville Square Historic District, Pensacola.*

admitted to the union as a slave state in 1845. At the time there were an equal number of slaves to white settlers. During the Civil War, Florida's location made it an ideal place to stash supplies for the Confederate army. Its capital, Tallahassee, was the only uncaptured Confederate capital east of the Mississippi.

Tallahassee was geographically the ideal state capital, located halfway between the two major pre-Civil War Florida cities of St. Augustine and Pensacola. It is located on the site of an Apalachee Indian village that de Soto visited in the early sixteenth century. It is a grand scale southern city whose splendor was rendered possible by cotton and timber fortunes. It was settled in the 1820s by members of prominent Carolina and Virginia families seeking new tracts of fertile lands. Many of these

families trace their lineage back to George Washington and Thomas Jefferson. The rich farm land of northern Florida continues to preserve an Old South flavor in the cities throughout the panhandle. Pensacola is the largest city of the area. It is one of the earliest coastal cities in North America, dating from 1559, when Tristan de Luna and a band of fifteen hundred settlers made camp at this superb natural harbor. Pensacola consequently clings tenaciously to the theory that it is the earliest settlement of white men. In 1959 it celebrated "America's first quadricentennial."

Coming under British rule in 1763, it became a Tory stronghold before and after the American Revolution. The Spanish got it back, but by then the British culture had dug in. When the Americans took over in the 1820s, they sent the war hero, Andrew Jackson, as the first provisional governor.

Pensacola immediately became an important naval yard, well-sheltered by Pensacola Bay. During World War I, it was the first naval aviation training base in the United States. Today this quiet city of oleanders and live oaks is the home base of the famed Blue Angels precision flying squadron.

Above: *Kennedy Space Center, Cape Canaveral, which sent the first men to the moon.*

Left: *Daytona Beach, once home of the Daytona Speedway.*

Reconstruction was as much an economic and political struggle in Florida as in the other southern states, but it suffered for a shorter time. A Yankee entrepreneur, Hamilton Disston, bought four million acres (6,250 square miles) of fertile swampland in the central part of the state for about twenty-five cents an acre, thus wiping out Florida's large war debt. Once the land was cleared, the riches of south Florida became evident. The center of development in the state suddenly shifted to the citrus belt and beachfront paradise of the lower part of Florida.

Perhaps southern Florida would have become a series of profitable farms separated by murky swamps had not the Gay 90s brought a number of northern speculators, who came south to play out their

167

One of the many beautiful houses in Key West.

fantasies. Henry Plant and Henry Flagler were two Connecticut "sharpies" out to make a quick buck. Both were interested in the trade potential of Latin America, both built railroad lines, and both wanted to create their own cities.

Flagler hired architects who went to Spain for the concept of his Ponce de Leon Inn at St. Augustine. The result was an exuberant style known as "Florida Baroque," which combines the most opulent aspects of Regency, Moorish, Spanish, and Italian architecture.

Plant's answer to this was the extravagant, one-fourth-of-a mile-long Tampa Bay Hotel, a Moorish, French, Victorian, and Japanese fantasy out of *The Arabian Nights*. This 1891 structure is a wonderland of six minarets, four cupolas, three domes, and keyhole arches.

Today Tampa is the third-largest city in Florida. The name came from the Calusa Indian term, "stick of fire," an apt name for the city which has become the capital of America's cigar industry. The neighboring Ybor City has a large Cuban population. Here are still tiled and mirrored restaurants reminiscent of the Mediterranean, where there is a faint aroma of garlic and saffron, and coffee is served thick and black as coal.

A few miles away, situated on the west coast of the Pinellas Peninsula, is St. Petersburg, created by a partnership between John Constantine Williams, the son of Detroit's first mayor – a notable figure with a beard to his belt buckle – and an exiled member of the Russian Imperial Guard with an elegant goatee and mustache, named Piotr Alexeitch Dementieff-Iverovsky. Today St. Petersburg has beautiful parks filled with banyan and oak trees. It is known as "the sunshine city," and it is a haven for retirees, shuffleboard, and spring baseball training camps.

Down the Gulf coast across the unpopulated wet-grass peninsula to Miami goes the Tamiami Trail, named for Tampa and Miami. The three-hundred-mile route is a procession toward the tropics in land, culture, and food. In the mid-1880s Thomas Edison arrived in this area in the town of Fort Myers to perform his first experiment for a filament in his incandescent lamp. Continuing other studies, he developed a dependable source of rubber in the United States, produced from hybrid golden rod. His experiments attracted both Henry Firestone and Henry Ford to the area. The town of Fort Myers gained

Above: *folk fishing off Hoover Dyke, near Clewiston.*

Below: *two men playing cards at the racetrack at Hialeah.*

notoriety when Edison offered to give the town a system of free electricity. The town fathers rejected the offer since they would have had to provide the wooden electrical poles, and they feared all the light might keep the cows awake.

Across the peninsula from Fort Myers, the robber barons discovered what would become the most famous jet-set watering hole in the Americas, Palm Beach. The city did not have particularly auspicious beginnings. The story goes that a Spanish ship ran aground with a large cargo of coconuts. Several centuries later the narrow, twenty-two mile strip of sand became an exotic palm-covered oasis of palatial estates and lavish parties. Contemporary society vies for mention in the city's "shiny sheet," the glossy daily paper.

South of Lake Okeechobee lie the Everglades, where the highest land is only a few feet above sea level. This one-hundred-mile-long, forty-mile-wide labyrinth of waterways threads through cypress and mangrove swamps, sawgrass, and shallow water, stretching all the way to the last fringe of coast. An aerial view will show "a watery garden" of haunting beauty, broken by patches of palms and oaks that wave gently above the grass. The whole Everglades is one of the largest national parks in America.

In the 1920s a section of road was hacked through

Left: *the elegant and splendid Breakers Hotel, Palm Beach, built in a Moorish style.*

Below: *Fort Jefferson, built in 1846, lies west of Key West on the isolated Dry Tortugas.*

Magnificent Art-Deco buildings overlook Miami Beach.

the Everglades to Miami. The deadly task involved "money, men, muck, machinery, misery and moccasins." This roadway and the railroad made Miami come to life. In 1896 Miami had a population of fifteen hundred; yet by 1920 it had grown to thirty thousand. Two wise investors bought sixteen hundred acres of mangrove swamp, which caused Will Rogers to quip, "They drained off the water moccasins and replaced them with hotels and New York prices." It is

one of the few twentieth-century cities to have created a unique style of its own, Miami Art Deco. It is also the home of the delicious stone crab claws, delicious meaty crab legs plucked off the living animals, who then grow other ones.

The southernmost city in the United States lies at the far edge of the Florida Keys on a four-mile-long by two-mile-wide strip of land between the Gulf of Mexico and the Atlantic Ocean, just ninety miles from Cuba. The overseas highway which connects Key West to the mainland is one of the most scenic roadways in

171

the world. In many places there is nothing but sparkling blue-green sea, blue sky, and sunshine. There are twenty-five islands in this archipelago, which stretches out in a wide crescent pointing southward from the mainland tip of Florida. De Soto named the islands "The Martyrs" because their shapes reminded him of men in torment. The name Key West means "Bone Key," a Spanish phrase deriving from the piles of human bones and debris washed ashore from shipwrecks.

In the early days Key West was a haven for pirates, buccaneers, and wreckers. They were a colorful combination of seafaring people from all over the world. One group, called "Conchs," consisted of English Bahamians with distinctive cockney accents, deserters from the Revolutionary War, New Englanders, Carolinians, and Cuban revolutionaries. When the United States acquired Florida in 1820, Commodore Porter was dispatched to clean up illegal activities. Wrecking gentry had been allowed to obtain

Above: *birds perching over the waters of the Dry Tortugas*

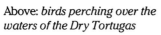

Left: *mangrove roots and "coon oysters."*

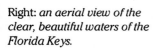

Right: *an aerial view of the clear, beautiful waters of the Florida Keys.*

Above: *Ernest Hemingway's office in his home on Key West, where he lived from 1931-40.*

Right: *fishing in the blood-red waters off Cedar Key in the Gulf of Mexico.*

licenses to "rescue" debris. Merchants built warehouses to house "found" cargoes of liquor, gold, and silver, which could then be sold for millions in profits. Houses and cisterns were built from salvaged wood. Fresh water was the most precious commodity in the city.

Gradually the make-up of the town shifted as lighthouses and steam vessels made navigation safer. The area remains an important strategic position for the military. Such characters as the late novelist Ernest Hemingway, playwright Tennessee Williams, and President Harry Truman liked to parade around the streets mingling with Cuban fishermen, tourists, and sailors amongst the night-blooming cereus, East Indian palm, and banyan trees.

South Florida, and especially the Keys, is an angler's paradise with acrobatic long-bodied snook leaping ten feet out of the water, the dolphin that changes color from blue to yellowish after it is caught, and the sailfish with its massive dorsal fin slicing through the water.

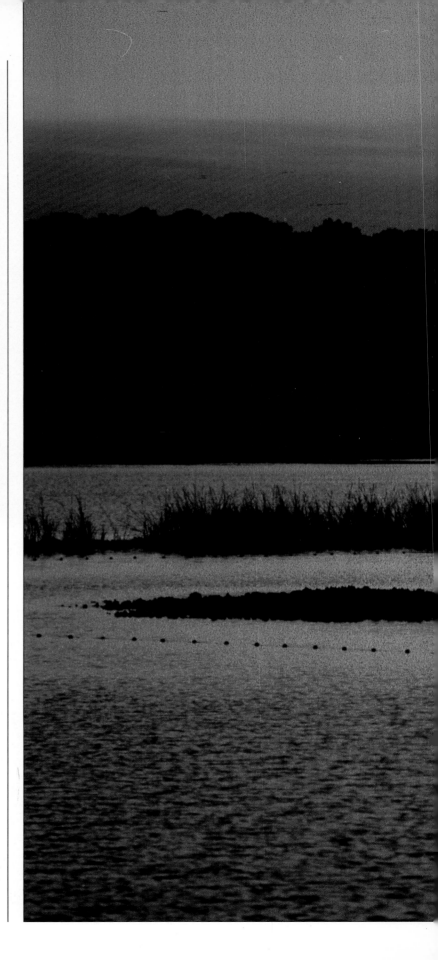